M000203790

RELIGION IN THE CLASSROOM

Dilemmas for Democratic Education

Jennifer Hauver James

WITH SIMONE SCHWEBER, ROBERT KUNZMAN,
KEITH C. BARTON, KIMBERLY LOGAN

Routledge
Taylor & Francis Group

NEW YORK AND LONDON

First published 2015
by Routledge
711 Third Avenue, New York, NY 10017

and by Routledge
2 Park Square, Milton Park, Abingdon, Oxon, OX14 4RN

Routledge is an imprint of the Taylor & Francis Group, an informa business

Library of Congress Cataloging-in-Publication Data

James, Jennifer Hauver.
    Religion in the classroom : dilemmas for democratic education / by Jennifer Hauver James with Simone Schweber, Robert Kunzman, Keith C. Barton, and Kimberly Logan.
        pages cm
    Includes bibliographical references and index.
    1. Religion in the public schools. 2. Religious education. I. Barton, Keith C. II. Title.
    LC107.J36 2015
    379.2'8—dc23
    2014022806

ISBN: 978-0-415-83296-0 (hbk)
ISBN: 978-0-415-83297-7 (pbk)
ISBN: 978-0-203-50744-5 (ebk)

Typeset in Bembo
by Apex CoVantage, LLC

For Sarah and Grace
I wish for you a world in which love leads the way

CONTENTS

Preface   *ix*

Acknowledgments   *xvii*

1 Beginnings   1

2 Toward Democratic Living and Learning   5

3 Navigating the Legal and Ethical Dimensions of Our Work   13

4 The Not-So-Hidden Curriculum of Religion in
Public Schools   23

5 Unpacking Narratives of Calling and Purpose in Teaching   39
Kimberly Logan

6 Fishing Below the Surface: Understanding the Role of
Religion in Student Learning   53
Simone Schweber

7 Reconsidering Religion in the Curriculum   61
Keith C. Barton

8 Talking with Students Who Already Know the Answer:
Navigating Ethical Certainty in Democratic Dialogue 79
Robert Kunzman

9 Continuing the Conversation 91

About the Contributors 97
Index 99

PREFACE

The aim of this book is to explore some of the ways religion figures into the experiences of teachers and students in classrooms. But essential to this exploration is an understanding of the vast and varied ways religion figures into our own lives and thinking *outside* of schools and classrooms.

Religion started for me on the pew of the Lutheran church. Sometimes my mother took us to the church in town, but just as often we attended her childhood church with our extended family in western Maryland. There my older cousin Elizabeth and I enjoyed playing hangman during the sermons, and I enjoyed tagging along with her to choir practice and youth group events. In the Lutheran church, I learned two things: 1) God loves me, 2) So I should love others. Beyond these core lessons, I remember traditions from my childhood—getting dressed up on Easter and searching for a hidden basket of goodies, setting up the nativity before Christmas, and counting down the days 'til Santa would visit on a ribbon that hung in our hallway. My introduction to religion was through a fairly progressive strand of Christianity, the Evangelical Lutheran Church of America. Lutheran was what "we" were; the identity marker gave me a sense of belonging, and the rituals we practiced brought (and still bring) me comfort.

It wasn't long, however, before I realized that not everyone did what "we" did or believed what "we" believed. In elementary school, I made a good friend (another Jenny) whose family was Jewish. She missed school occasionally to observe holidays I didn't. She taught me about Hanukkah and we debated who had the better deal—a present a night for eight nights or a bunch of presents all at once. Jenny introduced me to new foods that I, in turn, demanded my mother purchase too. Little by little my world grew. Then when I was ten, my mother remarried—to a Catholic Italian—and another door opened. I learned that even Christians had different beliefs and practices. One evening my mom took time to carefully explain why we would continue attending the Lutheran church, while my stepfather would not. With this marriage came a move to the outskirts of Washington, DC, and to a middle and high school more diverse than any I had attended before. I met people from all over the world, and of various religious (and non-religious) affiliations. I was introduced to Buddhism when a good friend showed me the shrine in her home, to Islam when another friend explained why we couldn't lunch together during Ramadan, to atheism when my best friend's family explained their abandonment of organized religion and a belief in God over dinner. My eyes were opened, and again, my world grew.

For the most part, as I grew, my faith accommodated my evolving commitments. In the early days of my teaching career, I worked at an elementary school that fed the high school I had attended. The school served almost exclusively poor, immigrant children whose cultural, linguistic, familial worlds were vast in variety and rich in beauty. Despite attending school in a large, wealthy district, these children were seemingly invisible, suffering policies shaped by administrators and politicians far removed from our reality. I began to see my community as it was lived by the children in my classroom and by their families, and I became highly critical of the very privilege and color blindness that had marked my own life for a quarter of a century. I became increasingly committed to issues of access and equity in schools and communities—commitments that were echoed in my church. As I grew increasingly critical of others' efforts to judge or exclude individuals and groups on the basis of sexual orientation, gender, race or class, I heard similar refrains from the pulpit. As I sought to advocate for women and children who were victims of abuse and neglect, so did my church. As I grew increasingly convinced of the relativism of truth and the importance of dialogue and humility, those in my family and my church encouraged and engaged in dialogue. For most of my life, my pastor was a gay man in a long-term relationship whose candor I found refreshing and inspiring. He believed that to grow in faith, we must ask questions. We were a congregation committed to serving the local (mainly immigrant) community and thinking and growing together in our efforts to live graciously. Whether my faith informed my commitments or I sought to make sense of my commitments through my faith, I can't be sure. But I found little tension between them.

When I moved to the Midwest with my former husband and my two daughters in the summer of 2006, however, my faith and my commitments clashed. Despite our best efforts, we struggled to find a church home. Lutheranism took a different spin in this new place than we were used to. We visited Episcopal churches, Methodist and Presbyterian churches, Congregational and Unitarian churches. Nowhere did we find others who shared both our grounding in Christianity and our commitments to social justice. The same struggle surfaced in my professional work. In my role as a teacher educator, I encountered many self-identified Christian students whom I struggled to understand; some who were bold enough to tell me quite directly that I wasn't "really" Christian. If I didn't see homosexuality as a sin, if I didn't understand the predetermined "natural" roles of men and women, if I didn't believe it was my job to save non-believers, if I didn't understand that birth control is an insult to God, well then I just wasn't Christian. This kind of talk mirrored what I had heard from preachers in churches all around me. Reasonable people could certainly disagree about these things, might discuss them, I thought. Yet I found few spaces in which disagreement and dialogue were welcome.

Eventually I came to the conclusion that maybe I wasn't "Christian." If, as those around me believed, Christians believed these things and acted in these ways, then I most certainly was (am) not. I stopped wearing a cross around my neck, stopped identifying as Christian. I became outwardly critical of religion in general as it became, for me, closely related to the judgment, exclusion and bigotry I had so long despised. My stomach turned when I overheard Bible studies in coffee shops, I turned off the TV when religious pundits started talking, I stopped reading the local paper for fear of running across some neighbor ranting about "family values." The brand of Christianity being flaunted was not one in which I wanted my family bathed. I became angry and critical of those around me. My crisis of identity led to a fair degree of social isolation and sadness.

Fortunately, my professional life gave me a space to start wrestling with the issues that beset me. I wanted to understand this Christianity my students claimed to know. I wanted to tease apart meanings of justice and tolerance. I knew that my students' and my own religion shaped, at least in part, our understandings of knowledge, truth, of ourselves and others, and I wondered what this might mean for who we become as teachers. I wanted to engage more fully the intersection of religion, politics and education. I wanted to understand the many ways religion is taken up and acted upon by those in schools.

In this book, you'll be introduced to many students,[1] who, over the years, have indulged my many questions and listened in return as I shared my own story. I conducted studies on pre-service teachers' religious understandings and their experiences of teacher education, their thinking about the teaching of controversial content, about relationships with students, and about their purposes as educators. Along the way I learned a great deal about the inherent overlap of teachers' professional and private selves, and of the wide variety of religious understandings held by those in education. I grew increasingly committed to putting religion squarely on the table for exploration as a teacher educator and as a scholar. And my understandings of democratic education deepened.

Today I live in Georgia with my two daughters. We occasionally attend the local ELCA church where we have met many wonderfully thoughtful people, who engage critically and humbly with the world around them. As participants in this faith community and in other spaces we've come to know, we read, reflect upon and discuss the social issues that plague our community and the ways that religion intersects with them (for better or for worse). I struggle still with the degree to which I consider myself "Christian," but I often revisit the lessons that shaped my upbringing: though I can't say I know for sure that love begins with

God, I have come to believe that we might all be better off if there were a little more of it in the world. And love, for me—whether romantic or platonic—if it is to be authentic and do good, must begin with understanding and acceptance on our own terms . . . with seeing and being seen.

I am currently a faculty member in social studies education at the University of Georgia, where I work with many students who are conservative and Christian in ways that I am not. I also work with students who span a wide variety of religious and non-religious positions. Knowing them continues to enrich my understanding of the world. I trust that though we may disagree on some core issues, my commitments to democracy and to justice demand that I model respect, humility, caution and hospitality in the face of difference. I encourage each of us to consider the consequences of our actions for others and our professional responsibility to respect and value all children. I strive every day to live in ways that are in accordance with my own commitments while being deeply respectful of others'. Striking this balance, I believe, requires walking humbly, working toward authenticity and in search of understanding—these themes you will find threaded throughout this book. Here, as is always the case, my professional and private selves are entwined. I share these pieces of my own story in order to shed light on the complexity of religious understanding and identity.

Religion is more than a scripted set of beliefs to which a group of people adheres. For many, religion is embedded in our lived experience in infinite and often invisible ways—informing our actions, framing our understandings and driving our fears. For those who are not religious, our deep convictions about the dangers and limits of religion may equally inform our actions and understandings. Reasons for the presence or absence of religion in an individual's life can be as varied and complex as the individuals themselves. Each of us has had our own religious education, made up of a unique set of experiences. These experiences have likely taught us a thing or two about what we believe, about what constitutes various religions, about the nature of religion and its place in public spaces. The origins of these understandings may be difficult to pinpoint— sometimes we can name specifically where we were introduced to a new idea or when our own thinking began to shift; sometimes we cannot. Regardless, these individual understandings come with us into the classroom, into our work as teachers with students, and into community with colleagues and families. They are part of us.

My experience as student and teacher has taught me two valuable lessons about the role of religion in schools. First, as suggested above, it is ever-present. Religion (our understandings and misunderstandings of it, our embrace of or resistance to it) enters the school doors as it is embodied in us, thus shaping our interactions with others, our interpretations of content, and embedded in the purposes we ascribe to our work. Our religious backgrounds—not just our beliefs, but our experiences with the religions around us—are part of our identities; a major part of how we make sense of the world, and they can help us understand others or stand in the way of understanding. And because of the historical connection between schools, religion and communities, religion (especially Protestant Christianity) is also present in the structures of schools—in the explicit recognition of holidays, in the academic calendar, in school assemblies, at sporting events and celebrations. Some of us may not notice just how present religion is in these ways, but Jewish students can quickly tell you that school events rarely take account of their holidays, Muslim students can explain that the daily schedule is not built around times for prayer, and atheist students can recite all the many times that devotional references to God are found in supposedly secular schools.

Second, though pervasive, the presence of religion in schools goes largely unexamined, and thus conversations about religion are rare. As educators we rarely discuss our religious backgrounds, and how those influence our teaching. We seldom mention religion to our students, except in occasional—and usually brief—explanations of social studies topics. Many teachers, in fact, are terrified to talk about religion in school—either their own religion or others'—because they think it somehow violates the separation of church and state, or they worry they might offend someone, or they just fear they don't know enough to speak about it intelligently. Unfortunately, beginning teachers rarely receive much guidance in these matters during their preparation programs. Few pre-service or in-service courses give teachers a chance to talk about their religious backgrounds and how those influence their ideas, nor do they address such topics as methods of teaching about religion, the influence of religion on students' understanding or ways of mediating students' differing religious convictions during the discussion of controversial issues. At most, teachers may sit through a lecture or two on constitutional issues surrounding religion and public schools—just enough to scare them without really helping them understand this complicated topic in any depth. I know from experience, though, that many beginning teachers would *like* to talk about religion, and that many others are put off by what they perceive as an anti-religious bias in their teacher education programs.

That religion is ever-present and yet unexamined is troubling to me. Silence can serve to perpetuate the myth of a line between religion and teaching and learning. "We can't talk about that here," says one student. "Religion is too personal and controversial," says a teacher. We might wish to sweep these issues under the rug—relegating religion to the private sphere where it makes us more comfortable. But in a pluralist, democratic society, we must be willing to engage difficult discussions about the role of religion in schools and classrooms. Our avoidance of religion, after all, does not mean that it goes away. If anything, an unwillingness to examine religion allows attitudes about it to run rampant, leading to marginalization and discrimination through the taken-for-granted nature of its presence or absence.

Throughout this book you will see that the contributing authors and I refer to democracy as a lens for understanding the role religion might play in public schools. When faced with a dilemma, we ask, what can a teacher do who is committed to democratic education? What are the consequences of various actions for democratic learning and living? Who is served by a particular pedagogical choice and who is not? These questions stem from our shared convictions about the promise of democratic education. We believe, as Parker (2003) does, that democratic education is not a neutral endeavor; rather, teaching is both a moral and political undertaking, one that "tries to predispose citizens to principled reasoning and just ways of being with one another" (p. xvii). Public schools, and public school teachers, we believe, bear the greatest responsibility for this work. Thus, the impetus for this book is to explore the intersection of religion, teaching and learning in light of these commitments.

Many books exist on the relationship between school and religion—covering such topics as school prayer, public funds for religious education, the permissibility of student religious clubs, larger political debates over textbooks and curriculum, and so on. Although, together, we touch on some of those topics here, they are not the chief concern. Rather, this book invites reflection and discussion around dilemmas at play in the lives and work of students and teachers in public schools. For instance, when and how should teachers encourage or accept talk of religious belief in the public school classroom? What happens when they do? How might students' and teachers' religious understandings inform their sensemaking about content? What conflicting ideas about the nature of the world arise when students and teachers work from frames of reference informed by different religious beliefs, or by none at all? How do teachers' own religious beliefs influence their teaching, consciously or unconsciously? These are just a few of the questions taken up here. In a few cases, we suggest possible answers. More often, we try to clarify and elaborate on the questions, and we explore the consequences of answering in different ways, so that each of us can reach our own conclusions about the messages we want to send to students, and the way we hope to prepare students for democratic life.

Organization of the Book

In the first three chapters, I set the stage for the ensuing discussion of the relationship between religion, teaching and learning. In Chapter 1, I share pieces of my story as a teacher educator and the dilemmas I encountered pertaining to religion, teaching and learning. My quest for understanding began in earnest in the classrooms and coffee houses I describe here, and so I offer these reflections as context for the work that follows. In Chapter 2, I lay bare my assumptions about the aims of democratic education. I argue that having a clear vision of where it is we hope to go is an important first step in moving forward with intention, so that we may think critically about our pedagogical choices and their implications for democratic living and learning in our classrooms. My understanding of the complex relationship between religion, dialogue and democracy informs the organization and content of the book, and so in this chapter I articulate both my theoretical stance and the ways this stance is reflected in the pages that follow. Chapter 3 explores the ethical and legal boundaries of our work as educators . . . but don't worry that you're going to have to sit through a dry-as-dust recounting of liturgical history. Instead, I begin with a brief overview of key constitutional principles and then turn to key take-aways that can help us, as teachers, to ethically navigate the intersection of religion, teaching and learning. In Chapter 4, I examine the pervasive, yet largely invisible role that religion plays in public schools. I argue that Protestantism continues to serve as the public school's moral compass and normative frame within which institutional and pedagogical decisions are made. Using democratic living as a litmus test for ethical action, I raise questions about the implications for diverse students.

Chapters 5 through 8 are authored by colleagues of mine, Kim Logan, Simone Schweber, Keith Barton and Rob Kunzman. These four individuals have indulged me countless times over the last six years in conversation about the intersection of religion, teaching and learning. They have been steady sources of patience, encouragement and insight . . . always willing to engage difficult questions, listen carefully and push my thinking in important ways. Because they are so smart, I have asked them to contribute to the conversation by telling bits of their own stories—taking up questions that reside at the intersection of religion, teaching and learning that are particularly interesting to them.

In Chapter 5, Kim attends to the many ways that teachers' religious understandings inform the purposes they ascribe to their work—sometimes subtly, sometimes explicitly. Specifically, she reports findings from a recent narrative inquiry of four female student teachers who self-identify as Christian and wrestle with the notion of teaching as a calling. In Chapter 6, Simone explores the ways in which students' religious understandings shape their learning experiences, helping us to think critically about making our classrooms spaces where students can be more fully present. In Chapter 7, Keith considers religion in the curriculum. He examines the necessity of helping students understand the complexity and diversity of world religions, grapple with the differing perspectives of religions with which they are less familiar, and understand the nature of religion as a social practice. And in Chapter 8, Rob explores how to engage "ethically certain" students in mutually respectful dialogue around sometimes difficult and controversial issues.

In the final chapter, I reflect on the dilemmas raised throughout the volume, and offer potential avenues for continued exploration of the intersection of religion, teaching and learning. Specifically, I discuss the importance of collaborative inquiry around the ways religion is present in schools and classrooms and the degree to which difference is welcome and engaged, explicit attention to the legal and ethical dimensions of teachers' work, and better understanding of democratic principles. I implore you to keep the conversation going!

I have high hopes for this book. First, I hope that you will find it to be thought-provoking. I hope that in reading it, you will let each issue sit with you, that it might push you to reflect on your own assumptions about religion and its role in teaching and learning. Perhaps it might challenge you to rethink your practices; or maybe you'll find it affirming as you recognize the capable ways you already engage the dilemmas presented. Further, I hope that reading it will inspire you to talk with others. I hope you will consider using it in a teacher inquiry group or sharing its content with K-12 students in order to invite their thinking on complex issues. If you're brave enough, you might even share it with parents and community members as a way of initiating important conversations about who "we" are and what sorts of changes might be necessary to make the "we" more authentic and inclusive. You might decide to continue the conversation initiated here in writing, research and scholarship—agreeing, disagreeing, expanding and deepening the lines of inquiry. Whatever comes of your reading, I hope that it will result in the making of more democratic spaces for us—and especially our children—to live and learn together.

Note

1. All students' names have been replaced by pseudonyms.

Reference

Parker, W.C. (2003). *Teaching democracy: Unity and diversity in public life.* New York: Teachers College Press.

ACKNOWLEDGMENTS

Five years ago, I sat at a wine and chocolate bar in Chicago with Bruce VanSledright puzzling aloud (again) about the many unexpected ways religion was playing a part in my teacher education classroom. With exasperation, I said, "It's making me crazy." He smiled (a rather knowing smile), picked up his glass of wine and said, "Write about it." I wasn't sure then that I had the courage or the clarity to write my way through the questions that plagued me. But when I sat down at the computer in the months that followed, Christina's story poured forth. It was, perhaps one of the easiest things I'd ever written. In hindsight, the ease was probably a result of having spent so long tossing it around in my head. Also, because it mattered to me a great deal that I should understand it better. That writing found its way into *Theory & Research in Social Education* in 2010 under the editorship of Pat Avery. It was entitled, "'Democracy is the devil's snare': Theological certainty and democratic teacher education." Immediately after it was published, I received a number of e-mails from educators across the nation—some sharing their own similar experiences, some challenging my interpretations, some thanking me for writing about a topic that seemed "taboo." I was invited to write an article for *Kappan*, to speak at Mercer University, and at several conference venues. I organized a session at an annual meeting of the College and University Faculty Assembly of the National Council for Social Studies entitled, "Is teaching open-mindedness pushing a liberal agenda?"—a panel of seven wonderfully smart colleagues whose stimulating dialogue still reigns in my memory as the best conference session ever. People lined the walls of the room, spilling out into the hallway. It became readily apparent to me then that I was not the only one puzzling about religion's place in the classroom.

Soon after, at a Starbucks coffee house—while attending yet another conference—Keith Barton suggested a book. We sketched various formats, discussed potential audiences, considered contributors . . . and *Religion in the Classroom: Dilemmas for Democratic Education* was born. The final product you hold in your hands has been a labor of love—a personal quest for understanding myself and the world better—and I certainly couldn't have done it alone. I am forever indebted to the many friends, family members and colleagues who have sat with me in coffee houses and wine bars, on screen porches and at the kitchen table, via Skype and e-mail—in an effort to make sense of the issues and questions captured in the pages that follow. Among them are the contributors themselves—Keith, Rob, Simone and Kim. Thank you for your brilliance, your capable pens and your partnership in this project. In addition, a sincere thank you to my friends and colleagues Kevin Meuwissen, Jessica Kobe, Walter Parker, Diana Hess, Pat Avery, Tim Slekar, Susan Iverson, Denise Morgan, Jen and Steve Cassata, Stephanie Fillman, Andy Gilbert and Alicia Crowe for your unending patience, insights and encouragement. To Naomi Silverman, Trevor Gori and all the folks at Routledge, thank you for all you've done to make this book a reality. A special thank you to the many students who shared yourselves and your time with me. I hope that I have honored your stories in their retelling. A little closer to home, I'd like to say thank you to my mother, Jane Curzio, to my brother and sister-in-law, Chris and Tracy Hauver, to Lizzy and Lawson Barnes, Gary James, Kay and Rich Melby . . . for perhaps too many holiday meals spent deep in conversation about my work. And to my partner, whose faith in and love for me astound me over and over . . . thank you for making my life the fullest it's ever been.

Finally, to the two beautiful young girls who have not only traveled this road with me, but have always been the inspiration for so much that I do as an educator and scholar, Sarah and Grace, thank you for sacrificing time with me so that this book could get written. I hope some day it will make you proud.

1

BEGINNINGS

In the spring of 2008, I had an encounter that—though I didn't know it at the time—would change me forever. It was nothing less than a crisis of identity, an experience that shook my foundation and pushed me to begin to see anew myself, others and the world we shared. It is in that moment that this story begins.

★★★

Christina was an undergraduate student in my early childhood social studies methods course. A self-identified "Biblical Christian" who attended a local congregational mega-church, she was slightly older than the typical undergraduate education student, and married. In her own words, she had recently "recommitted her life to Jesus Christ, her Lord and Savior."

Christina was one of 27 students in the course that spring whom I invited to think with me about democratic living and learning as aims of social studies education. Preparation for civic life is a goal embedded in educational vision and mission statements across the nation and a central theme of social studies curricula and standards. As has been my practice for some time, I asked the students in the class to reflect on their own experiences inside and outside of schools in order to answer two questions: "What does it mean to be a 'good' citizen?" and "How do we come to understand for ourselves what good citizenship entails?" The purpose of this assignment is twofold: 1) to push students to consider their private understandings of citizenship as they have evolved through personal experience; and 2) to set the state for our shared sense-making of this question in relation to our work with children. They were tasked to write a short paper in response to these prompts before coming to class to dialogue with their peers.

Christina began her paper this way:

> If our goal is to manifest a definition of a "good citizen" in respect to a world that harbors not even one of them, we fail to see our innate need to recognize our common condition as humans, which is inherently that opposite of good . . . Psalm 14:1 . . . "there is no one who does good . . ." Romans 3:12 . . . "there is no one who does good, not even one . . ." Obviously it is apparent that my definition of a good citizen does not exist because a good citizen does not exist.

Later she addressed democratic citizenship more specifically, writing:

> In an act to be "democratic," we are limiting the views of those who state that there is absolute truth and an absolute order. It limits the option that there is a right path to take and it eliminates the Author who designed it in the first place.

Christina went on in her writing to depict a scene where a fly grows increasingly knotted up in a web that she weaves of her own confusion (moral relativism), ultimately trapping herself for the spider. She likened this scene to the human condition in which we "weave a tangled web" and create a "fleshy feast" for Satan. "Democracy," she wrote, "is the devil's snare."

Christina was the first aspiring teacher I ever met who so eloquently and vehemently opposed democracy. I admit that I hardly knew how to respond to the paper she submitted. That day in class, I invited her to share her opinions so they might be included in our shared sense-making about citizenship. She did so. Then, after a few subtle exchanges of glances, students began to ask questions such as "What do you mean?" and offer examples of good Samaritans from the local community to challenge her claim. Some students seemed generally interested in understanding Christina's point of view, while others seemed annoyed by her participation. Christina, however, quickly retreated, saying, "Each of us can believe what we want. I'm used to being the outsider and not having my voice heard." For the remainder of the class period, Christina withdrew from conversation. After class when I asked her to expound upon her last statement, she shared with me that throughout her time in the teacher education program, she had felt ostracized for her religious beliefs. "You all preach democracy and tolerance," she said, "but you're not tolerant of me."

In the days that followed, I talked with a number of colleagues in the hope of making sense of this encounter with Christina. Where had she learned that listening to alternative viewpoints must mean betraying her faith? I wondered. How did she understand the meaning of the word tolerance? The relationship between diversity and democracy? In what ways had her religious understandings played out in the teacher education classroom before and how had other instructors responded? What was I to make of a future teacher who claimed to want to work in public schools with diverse children, but who rejected the idea that there could be more than one way to understand the world? Reactions from my peers were sharp and varied. My closest colleague advised me to return the paper giving it zero credit. Christina had, she reasoned, not answered the questions posed. She had rejected the questions out of hand. Another colleague suggested that I try to counsel Christina out of the program since she clearly didn't demonstrate the respect for difference necessary to work in public education. Yet another colleague said he thought Christina was just going through a phase and I shouldn't take it too seriously. Most often, though, my colleagues were disinclined to discuss the issue. "Leave it alone," I often heard. "Don't touch that," others said. My department chair at the time recommended that I not "poke that bear."

None of these suggestions sounded quite right to me, but I was at a loss for how to move forward. I was deeply troubled by Christina's claims about democracy, yes. But I was equally concerned about her feeling ostracized within the teacher education program and her accusations that those of us claiming to be "democratic educators" were acting in hypocritical ways. This brief encounter pushed me to think carefully about the purposes I ascribed to my work, about my practice and about Christina's experiences of both. Unable to resolve the tensions I felt, I did the only thing I could think to do: I approached Christina and asked if she'd be willing to talk with me. I assumed that talk might help us to push past the anger and resentment that had bubbled up in our last class session together, that perhaps I could help to clear up any miscommunication about the assignment, figure out how to make her feel more comfortable in the class, and sort out my own misgivings about the role religious belief ought to play in a teacher education classroom.

Christina was kind enough to meet with me, first in my office, then at a local diner, eventually with a couple of other students who shared her beliefs and wanted to share their thoughts with me. In these discussions I began to see myself in relief—through Christina's eyes. Though I had long identified as a Christian, having grown up in the Lutheran church, Christina pointedly questioned my Christianity. She believed that I had strayed, bought into a "light" version of religion that suited my more worldly desires. She explained to me what a real Christian is and does, and how she prayed that I would return to the fold. I, in turn, tried to help Christina see the error of her ways, the limits of her understanding and the need for her to be more open-minded. In hindsight, each of us was trying to save the other. We realized, over time, that we were both on a mission and that those missions were colliding. We agreed that maybe the best way to reach greater understanding was not talking, really, but listening. And so our conversations shifted away from telling, toward asking. We asked each other about our own religious upbringings and understandings, we inquired as to how the other understood words and phrases like "open-mindedness" and "tolerance," reflected on shared experiences of her teacher education program and puzzled together about how to bridge what sometimes appeared to be unbridgeable chasms between us.

I am grateful to Christina for engaging me in these sometimes difficult conversations. I am forever indebted to her for allowing me to use the muddle of our misunderstandings as a space for inquiry. Christina wasn't the only one. Many former students over the years—Christian, Jewish, atheist, agnostic alike—have shared pieces of themselves with me, demonstrating a willingness to learn with me, to grow in our understanding of one another and of how our religious understandings intersect with our experiences of learning to teach.

In the months and now years that have followed since that first encounter in our methods classroom, I have gained tremendous respect for Christina and others who share their deep religious convictions. I have grown in my appreciation for the relationship between diversity and democracy. I have learned to see myself through new lenses and to walk more cautiously and humbly in the world. And I have come to believe in the incredible power of talk for bridging difference and growing our capacity for community.

I am unfinished and becoming . . . There are many questions that remain for me about the relationship between religion, teaching, learning and democracy, and this book is my effort to continue the conversation. As someone I love very much likes to say, "We study who we are—to know ourselves better—in hopes of becoming more fully human." The pages that follow are exactly that—my quest for understanding. In it, I share what I have learned about religion and teaching since that spring in 2008. I have invited others to contribute their own expertise to the book to attend more fully to the range of questions that plague me still. At the outset of each chapter, I have included guiding questions that I hope you, the reader, will take up with me and with others. I do so in the hope that we might come to know ourselves and each other better, to think deeply and critically about the sort of world we hope to inhabit, and how our work as educators might make such a world more possible.

2

TOWARD DEMOCRATIC LIVING AND LEARNING

Guiding Questions:

What do we mean by democratic education?
How are democratic living and learning related?

We in the United States generally agree that schools ought to be in the business of preparing students for engagement in civic life. We do not always agree on exactly what that preparation might involve or what mature civic engagement entails. Moving beyond the rhetorical space of what schools *should* do treads on highly political ground that most educators and policy makers wish to avoid. Throw religion in the mix and we are even less likely to touch it. Often, to avoid political minefields, we settle on rather impoverished notions of civic education (striving for increased voter turnout or higher scores on national civics exams) rather than on the difficult demands of preparing young people for respectful and responsible living in a diverse society. But if our aims are small in scope, we shouldn't be surprised when the payouts are also limited. Volunteerism and voting may be slightly up in this country, but so too is political polarization and avoidance of cross-cutting dialogue. Less than a quarter (23%) of adults in the United States engage in discussion of political issues (Mutz, 2006), a phenomenon that researchers say results from people choosing to live in increasingly ideologically homogeneous communities (Bishop, 2008) and a growing aversion to conflict over political issues (Hibbing & Theiss-Morse, 2002).

What would it mean to hammer a stake in the landscape of civic education—a stake that then serves as a reference point for designing and assessing policy and practice? That is the goal of this chapter. In recent years, I have worked hard to articulate what I mean by democratic education, looking through time and space to others who have sought to do the same. I have read widely and talked with a great many self-identified democratic educators from around the world in my quest for clarity. I have visited schools in multiple European countries, across the United States and in Canada. I have spoken at length with colleagues from Singapore, Japan, China, Australia, Central America and the Middle East in the hope of better understanding how others think about preparing students for participation in democratic life. Some of the most interesting conversations I've had have been with educators in non-democratic countries, who, because they have strikingly different conceptions of citizenship and civics than I do, have helped me crystallize my own thinking.

Of course, any discussion of democratic education is necessarily laden with particular ideas about what constitutes "good citizenship" and a "good society." The one I lay before you here is an ideal, born of understandings and commitments I have gleaned from my many experiences. I offer it here as both a starting place and an end goal, because before we can thoughtfully consider the dilemmas of religion, teaching and learning, we must know where it is we are trying to go. As the old Chinese proverb says, if you want to reach your destination, make sure each step you take is in that general direction. Making sure that we are headed in the direction of democratic learning requires a clear sense of what such learning might look like in the end.

Democratic Education as a Path to Civic Mindfulness

I have come to understand democratic education as a movement toward *mindfulness—mindfulness* meaning awareness and intention (from the Old English translation); and an ability to move beyond the self into greater communion with others (the Buddhist construct of "enlightenment"). The idea of mindfulness captures two central elements of student development theory that can also be found in contemporary conversations about civic education. The first of these is that civic maturity involves a shift away from egocentrism toward *mutuality*.

Mutuality

Mutuality in democratic education means that "it is in the interest of all to care as much about each other's self-development as one's own" (Brookfield & Preskill, 1999, p. 12). Because there is an inherent symbiotic relationship between an individual and her larger community, mutuality is foundational to a healthy democracy. My right to speak my mind, or to practice a religion of my choosing, depends on the right of others to do the same. In other words, if one person or group's rights can be taken away, so can another's. It's the very presence of small, private "publics" that keep the necessary balance in place to ensure freedom for all (Parker, 2003).

Essential to mutuality is approaching interactions with humility and caution. It requires that we admit we cannot ever know what it is like to walk in another's shoes and that we acknowledge the ever-present possibility that we may be wrong

(Parker, 2003, pp. 92–93). Parker (2003) writes, "If I am cautious when listening and responding, I will engage carefully so that I am not denying or dismissing the validity of the insider's point of view, nor even appearing to do so" (p. 93). Humility and caution are necessary only because we cannot ever truly escape the private spaces we inhabit and the ways they shape our knowing. Competent participation in a civic space, then, involves,

listening as well as talking, striving to understand points of view different from one's own, challenging ideas and proposals rather than persons, admitting ignorance, slowing the rush to decision so as to clarify or reframe the problem or gather more information . . . even appreciating the principle attributed to Voltaire: "I disapprove of what you say, but I will defend to the death your right to say it."

(Parker, 2003, pp. 87–88)

Listening, however, is a willful enterprise. Individuals can, and often do, refuse to open themselves up to new and different ideas; to see others as having important contributions to make to a conversation; to listen. Engaging in genuine listening across difference means we must willingly set aside our deeply held convictions long enough to consider those of others. Though we can never truly abandon the lenses we use to view the world, democratic citizenship demands that we participate in the public sphere with a commitment to identifying a mutually agreeable course of action. If we take the notion of mutuality as central to mature democratic citizenship, then an interpersonal skill like authentic, active listening, and an appreciation for its importance, are critical to democratic education.

Strong Internal Foundation

Also necessary for civic maturity is movement away from blind trust in external authorities toward confidence in one's own ability to make decisions, or the development of a *strong internal foundation*. An individual who has a firm foundation trusts her internal voice (Baxter Magolda, 2001). Such a person "[knows] herself well enough to determine when to make things happen versus when to let them happen, to live life on her own terms" (p. 274). Civic educators call this move toward a strong internal foundation the development of individual "autonomy" (Barber, 2003, p. 232). Some scholars describe this as a process of "reclaiming the self," suggesting that the journey of moral development is a quest for knowing, accepting and naming oneself (Belenky, Clinchy, Goldberger, & Tarule, 1986). Siddle Walker and Snarey (2004) say that naming ourselves, particularly against culturally constructed conceptions of who we ought to be, is an indicator of maturity. In this way, naming oneself is evidence of agency:

Agency is the individual's ability to process and structure his or her life experiences . . . Because American society devalues people of color, African

Americans have formed a sense of agency that relies upon their self-perceptions, rather than the images depicted by the dominant culture. The elements of agency—self-reflection, consistency, personal responsibility, pride, decision-making ability, self-reliance—are characteristics that allow African American children, youth, and adults to rise above and succeed in adverse conditions.

(p. 10)

General agreement exists about the importance of a strong internal foundation for engaging respectfully, responsibly and in ways that honor ourselves and others within the larger world. A diminished sense of self, in fact, can get in the way of our willingness to participate in spaces where others are likely to disagree or challenge our ideas. If I know and trust myself, I am more likely to engage with others uninhibited by fear and insecurity. I am ready to listen, to grant others the benefit of the doubt, and I feel confident in my voice as I speak.

A strong sense of self also means that I understand I am a product of my lived experiences and that my identity evolves over time in relation to those experiences. If my identity and ideas are fluid, it is likely that others' are too. In this way, my knowledge of self helps to shape how I understand and relate to others. If I grant that others' ideas reflect their unique experiences, and that the context of our interaction likely shapes how those ideas are conveyed, I can approach our interaction with greater humility and caution. A strong sense of self, then, facilitates understanding of others, and makes possible mature, mutual, reciprocal and *authentic* civic relationships. As Ricoeur (1992) argues, "The autonomy of the self will appear then to be tightly bound up with solicitude for one's neighbor and with justice for each individual" (p. 18).

A shift toward mature democratic citizenship, measured by our ability to participate in "we" thinking and the development of a strong internal foundation, is facilitated by a shift in the locus of control over the construction of knowledge (as we develop a stronger internal foundation) and a move toward more sophisticated understandings of the nature of knowledge itself (as we grow in understanding of ourselves and others). Learning to trust oneself as a constructor of knowledge involves a movement away from *received* knowledge (receiving from an external authority) toward having faith in oneself to construct knowledge (Belenky et al., 1986). Moving toward a more sophisticated understanding of the nature of knowledge involves a shift from *duality* (knowledge as black and white), through *multiplicity* (many ways to understand something), through *relativism* (belief that anything goes), toward *commitment* (ability to sort through arguments and make choices that align with one's own commitments) (Perry, 1981).

Democratic and civic education scholars emphasize cognitive sophistication as integral to mature democratic citizenship; they argue that mature citizens have an appreciation for the provisional nature of knowledge and the tentativeness of political judgment (Gutmann & Thompson, 2004). Mature citizens understand that communities must make the best decisions that they can in a given set of circumstances and with the existing membership. Making such decisions requires not only an ability to engage sophisticated cognitive activities such as reasoned critical, creative and flexible thinking, but also requires a shift away from dualisms toward an understanding of knowledge as constructed, incomplete and always provisional.

Democratic Living and Learning in Schools

Some of the most "teachable moments" that I've had cropped up when I merely provided space for students' natural curiosity and interest to guide us. Take, for instance, the afternoon when I'd had enough of students bickering over pencils in the classroom and asked for their help to resolve our shortage problem. Or when, as a classroom community, we thought together about how best to comfort a child among us who was suffering a great loss. Or the time when we puzzled together about how to fix a broken leg on our art table. In each of these instances, life confronted us with its very real demands and we rose—together—to meet them. In each was a lesson—about decision-making in the face of scarce resources, about empathy and friendship, about design, materials and mathematics—lessons embedded in the world around us, made interesting because they were relevant. In each of these shared challenges was also an opportunity to practice democratic living. Because I was clear about my goals, I was able to approach each situation with intention, striving to foster students' sense of self, their ability to sit with complexity, and their capability to engage respectfully with others. These goals shaped the pedagogical moves I made—the questions I asked, the role I assumed, the expectations I had for students.

Rather than seeing a dispute over a shortage of pencils in the classroom as getting in the way of learning, for example, I was able to refashion it as an opportunity *for* learning. I reminded students of the community they said they wanted us to be, the responsibilities each of us agreed we had to one another. I posed the problem and asked for solutions. I created space for free-flowing dialogue among students, placing myself in the role of facilitator rather than expert. I helped them to see the similarity between our pencil problem and some of the issues adults face in larger communities. I drew attention to the ways they interacted with each other over the issue, affirmed each individual's experience and position, and worked to ensure that students thought deeply about each solution put on the table.

It was not a lesson I intended to teach that day. I had not identified relevant standards (though there were, of course). It was not dictated by my pacing guide and would not be assessed on the end-of-quarter test. I gave the issue time because I believe that it is in the informal spaces of togetherness we share in classrooms that democratic learning is most powerful. The pencil problem was pressing. It frustrated each and every one of us. It led us to accuse each other of foul play, made us feel protective of our belongings and threatened to disrupt our community. I could have easily replenished the supply of pencils over and over in an effort to make the problem go away. I could have reprimanded students for not taking better care of our classroom materials. I could have had students put their names on their pencils and held them individually accountable for their property. But we would have missed an opportunity to construct our own resolution to our shared problem, to think together, to grow in understanding of how others experience a phenomenon we think we understand. We would have missed a chance to walk the difficult road of living—democratically.

My invitation to Christina to share her opinions as part of our in-class discussion of citizenship was done with similar aims in mind. Knowing the conviction in Christina's writing, I might have shied away from making space for her perspective as part of our class dialogue. She'd certainly learned from previous experience that her voice was marginal. She might not have even pressed to be included. But I felt sure that despite my own discomfort and uncertainty about how it would go, there were good reasons to plow forward. Christina had a right, like all of my students, to share her thoughts as part of our collective sense-making. And her classmates—all of us, I hoped—would be better off for having to wrestle with diverse points of view, especially those rooted in religion, as it gave us the very real opportunity to discuss the role of private belief in public school discourse. I would handle the situation differently today than I did six years ago. Though my goals were clear, I was unprepared for what transpired. Talking with students afterwards, reading and reflecting on my practice helped me to see where I'd mis-stepped and what I might do differently next time in order to foster a dialogic space that leads to greater understanding, tolerance and respect.

Schools and classrooms, as public spaces, are crucial contexts for engaging students in democratic living (Dewey, 1996 [1916]; Parker, 2003). But again, as educators, we can only make the most of the opportunities schools provide when we are clear about the democratic goals we hope to achieve.

Toward Democratic Living and Learning

As conceived here, democratic learning goes well beyond traditional notions of civics that aim to teach children about the three branches of government or how a bill becomes a law. It is not satisfied with participation limited to dropping cans in a food drive box or stopping off at the polls after work. It expands the vision of mature citizenship to include mutuality and a strong internal foundation. It aims to prepare young people who see themselves as capable agents with purpose and conviction, who are able to sit comfortably with complexity and work collectively with diverse others to address issues facing their communities. The definition assumes (as I do) that democratic societies must be spaces where individuals can rise above their private interests to engage responsibly and respectfully with others for a common good.

Democratic learning and democratic living are inextricably intertwined. We cannot expect to prepare students to be active, respectful, thoughtful citizens if they have few opportunities to practice such engagement in schools. The definition offered here can (and I believe should) serve as a litmus test against which we can evaluate the potential consequences of pedagogical and political choices we might make. No instructional approach is inherently democratic. Nor does any method necessarily result in democratic learning. Discussion-based practice is believed to grow students' appreciation for a diversity of perspectives, their ability to engage in attentive, respectful listening, and their appreciation for difference (Brookfield & Preskill, 1999). But as a visit to any local school will make clear, discussion is employed in many ways. We might ask of the teaching and learning we observe there: what is the nature of the classroom-based discussions being conducted? Do students feel free to share their voices and arrive at their own meanings? Or do teachers seem to want students to leave with particular understandings of the content under study? When students are invited into discussion, who sets the agenda? How are differences of opinion resolved? What counts as a "successful" talk? For instruction to have democratic value, the teacher must approach it with specifically democratic aims. Again, knowing where we hope to go allows us to move with intention and reflect with purpose.

I am not naïve about the demands such a conception of democratic education puts on educators. Nor am I blind to the challenges we face in working toward it. Even as we grow clearer and more resolved in our educational mission, walking the road will not always be easy. We must be vigilant, ever looking for spaces where democratic living is possible and raising critical questions where it seems not to be. I would argue that such vigilance is particularly important in today's school climate where increasing standardization and top-down, high-stakes accountability measures rule the day. Here, democratic living and learning struggle to find a foothold. Here, bold teachers with clear aims are essential. We must carve space for democratic living and stave off the deleterious consequences of competition and control.

As we'll see in the pages that follow, when religion, teaching and learning intersect, many dilemmas arise. Individuals and groups feel marginalized by practices others in their community find "normal" and "right." Aspiring teachers' "call" to teach is entwined with their Christian call to love and serve others. Students' religious understandings shape their sense-making of content and their interactions with others in subtle, sometimes unconscious ways. Parents insert themselves into the lives of schools demanding the inclusion or exclusion of activities and materials they believe to be in conflict with their religion. Teachers' fear keeps them from teaching about religion, but their silence only affirms students' suspicion that religion is "too hot to touch."

In Chapter 3, we'll see that the questions arising from these dilemmas can sometimes be resolved by looking to the law. But often the particulars of practice—what to do and how, what is a right course of action and for whom—remain awfully fuzzy. Sorting out what to do is made even more complicated by pressure to stay on script rather than open space for inquiry and dialogue, by uneasy community members who prefer we transmit particular truths to students rather than grow their capacity to construct meanings of their own, by our own and others' fear of difference and sometimes, by ignorance . . . about the law, about the critical relationship between diversity and democracy, and about others. Sometimes we, ourselves, are unable to see the barriers we face because they have become as natural and normal to us as the air we breathe. Having a clear goal in mind is helpful for assessing the likely consequences of various choices for students' democratic learning, but it will not always be enough.

In this chapter, I have offered a starting place—a vision of democratic education that aims to move young people toward mutuality and a strong internal foundation—toward civic mindfulness. I argue that, when confronted with dilemmas like those listed above, we ought to ask ourselves whether our response will facilitate or hinder democratic learning, and move with caution. In the next chapter, I share some of the lessons I've learned about the legal and ethical boundaries of our work in schools in hopes of further clarifying the need for a clear vision of our civic mission and of the role of religion in reaching it. Beginning with Chapter 5, my colleagues join the conversation and we jump headlong into the messiness of religion in the classroom. Ready?

References

Barber, B.R. (2003). *Strong democracy: Participatory politics for a new age.* Berkeley, CA: University of California Press.

Baxter Magolda, M.B. (2001). *Making their own way: Narratives for transforming higher education to promote self-development.* Sterling, VA: Stylus Publishing.

Belenky, M.F., Clinchy, B.M., Goldberger, N.R., & Tarule, J.M. (1986). *Women's ways of knowing: The development of self, voice, and mind.* New York, NY: Basic Books.

Bishop, B. (2008). *The big sort: Why the clustering of like-minded Americans is tearing us apart.* New York: Houghton Mifflin.

Brookfield, S.D., & Preskill, S. (1999). *Discussion as a way of teaching: Tools and techniques for democratic classrooms.* San Francisco, CA: Jossey-Bass.

Dewey, J. (1996). The democratic conception in education. In W.C. Parker (Ed.), *Educating the democratic mind* (pp. 25–44). Albany, NY: SUNY Press. (Original work published in 1916.)

Gutmann, A., & Thompson, D. (2004). *Why deliberative democracy?* Princeton, NJ: Princeton University Press.

Hibbing, J., & Theiss-Morse, E. (2002). *Stealth democracy: America's beliefs about how government should work.* New York: Cambridge University Press.

Mutz, D.C. (2006). *Hearing the other side: Deliberative versus participatory democracy.* New York: Cambridge University Press.

Parker, W.C. (2003). *Teaching democracy: Unity and diversity in public life.* New York: Teachers College Press.

Perry, W.G., Jr. (1981). Cognitive and ethical growth: The making of meaning. In A.W. Chickering & Associates, *The modern American college: Responding to the new realities of diverse students and a changing society* (pp. 76–116). San Francisco, CA: Jossey Bass.

Ricoeur, P. (1992). *Oneself as another.* Chicago, IL: University of Chicago Press.

Siddle Walker, V., & Snarey, J.R. (2004). *Race-ing moral formation: African American perspectives on care and justice.* New York: Teachers College Press.

3

NAVIGATING THE LEGAL AND ETHICAL DIMENSIONS OF OUR WORK

Guiding Questions:

What guidelines exist for helping us navigate dilemmas about religion in the classroom? What do we do when the guidelines aren't enough?

One thing my encounter with Christina made clear to me was the limit of my own knowledge about the legal and ethical boundaries of my work as a teacher. Though I had been a teacher for over a decade, worked with hundreds of students in a variety of educational settings, even been awarded two graduate degrees in education, I couldn't recall a single time when I'd had the opportunity to learn about what the law said was "right" and "fair" regarding religion in the classroom.

I'd asked the question before. There was Farhi, a third-grade student I taught early in my career. His family refused to allow him to be exposed to music except as part of religious observances. They insisted that I was to refrain from playing music in the classroom, keep Farhi from celebrations where music would be played, and find an alternative to music class. Wasn't music a mandatory subject in our state? Did Farhi's family have a right to dictate whether I played music in my classroom?

A couple of years later, I taught a little girl named Shara. She very clearly struggled with a learning disability—something her prior teachers had documented well and tried to secure services to address. My own efforts went the way of others when Shara's father came to the school and explained that, as a girl, Shara had no real need for an education. She was only enrolled in the school because the state mandated it. He had no intention of signing paperwork for her to receive additional services at school since he found the whole idea of her education preposterous. His perspective—a mixture of personal and cultural beliefs, justified in his mind by religion—came as a great shock to me. Though Shara's father didn't see the value in her education, I certainly did, and as a school employee I felt obligated to do what I could to help her succeed.

Parents can and do insert themselves into schools when they believe their children's experience may violate their private right to practice the religion of their choosing. Sometimes parents advocate for their own children, but often their demands implicate other children as well. Take the parent who, in the year after *Harry Potter and the Sorcerer's Stone* was published, demanded that all copies of the book be banned from our school and classroom libraries. She was adamant that its magical content was inappropriate for young children and used her Christian belief system to justify her arguments. Or a parent I met through a local preschool who insisted that leading young children in yoga—a practice she believed to be religious in nature—was inappropriate. Despite the teacher's articulation about the benefits of yoga for concentration, peacefulness and gross motor strength, the parent demanded that she stop . . . threatening to have her daughter reassigned to another classroom if she did not. Where does a student's or family's right to practice their religion stop and the school's right to privilege diversity and respect for the individual and for difference begin?

Christina's paper, in which she called on the Bible to justify her argument that there was no such thing as a "good" citizen, and her subsequent claims about democracy being the devil's work were in some ways no different than these earlier experiences I'd had with students. Christina, and other students after her, often disengaged from class discussions and debates, refused to consider alternative points of view, and used religious conviction as justification for doing so. It seemed to me, however, that I had an obligation to help prepare Christina for her work, just as I had an obligation to teach music to Farhi and provide educational services to Shara. Christina would be interning and student teaching in public schools, where she claimed she wanted to work one day. Certainly, she had a right to her beliefs and to articulate them. But didn't I, as a teacher educator, have a responsibility to consider the students Christina would one day teach?

Vexed by these questions, I turned to colleagues for answers about how to navigate these tricky waters, just as I had turned to them so many times before. But as I explained in the introduction, my colleagues seemed just as clueless as I was. Either there weren't any clear-cut rules about the role of religion in the classroom or, if there were, we certainly didn't know them. And yet, we felt comfortable making such recommendations as failing Christina on her assignment and counseling her out of the program . . . moves that, to me, seemed risky without a greater understanding of their legal and ethical implications. Ultimately (because I continued to nag my department chair), we invited three university lawyers to visit our faculty meeting and talk with us about students' and teachers' rights as they related to religious belief. It was a start. What I soon realized, however, was that though there are some clearly defined boundaries, there is also a lot of gray area when it comes to knowing the right thing to do when religion comes knocking at the classroom door. I am no constitutional historian. Nor am I a lawyer. I have, however, spent a great deal of time reading and talking with others in hopes of gaining greater clarity about the legal and ethical boundaries of my work as an educator. In what follows, I share what I have come to know in the hope of making the waters a little less murky for others.

Constitutional Guidelines

In 1791, the First Amendment was adopted as part of the U.S. Constitution. It includes the phrase, "Congress shall make no law respecting an establishment of religion, or prohibiting the free exercise thereof." As argued by James Madison, the Amendment's fiercest advocate, "Who does not see that the same authority which can establish Christianity, in exclusion of all other Religions, may establish with the same ease any particular sect of Christians, in exclusion of all other Sects?" (*Memorial and remonstrance*, June 20, 1785). Though Madison had no problem with religion in general, he strongly opposed its establishment at both the state and federal levels. His intent, it seems, was to protect "evangelicals and other religious dissenters who challenged the established churches of the colonial period" (Irons, 2007, p. 3).

The two clauses regarding religion in the First Amendment—the *Establishment Clause* and the *Free Exercise Clause*—serve as the basis upon which religious freedom is guaranteed in this country (Haynes & Thomas, 2007). Though these clauses have been the subject of much debate before the Supreme Court in recent decades, I have come to understand that there is some general agreement about their application that can come in handy when trying to make sense of the questions that afflict me about religion and teaching.

Establishment

The Establishment Clause ostensibly forbids the establishment of religion by the government. What this means exactly is a little tricky to nail down, but in 1971, the Supreme Court heard the landmark *Lemon v. Kurtzman* case, which has served as a reference point for considering the constitutionality of state interference in religious activities ever since. Alton Lemon was a Pennsylvania teacher who filed the case against David Kurtzman, acting Superintendent of the Department of Public Instruction in the State of Pennsylvania. Lemon claimed that the recent "Non-Public Elementary and Secondary Education Act" (passed in 1968) violated the Constitution because it directed public funds to private schools. On June 28 of that year, the Supreme Court ruled (eight to one) in favor of Mr. Lemon.

From this decision came a set of criteria called the "Lemon Tests," which continue to serve as a useful reference point for evaluating the lawfulness of government-sanctioned religious activity. Given that public schools, and by extension, public school teachers, are part of the state, these three tests can be useful guides for assessing the constitutionality of choices we make in schools as well. First, we must ask whether the activity in question has a true secular or civic purpose. Second, we must evaluate the degree to which the primary effect of an activity either advances or inhibits religion. Third, we need to consider whether the activity manages to avoid excessive state entanglement with religion.

Let's consider a teacher's decision to erect a Christmas tree in her classroom in December. Right? Wrong? Constitutional? Unconstitutional? It depends. According to the first Lemon Test, we have to ask whether putting up the Christmas tree is intended for truly secular, civic (and educational) purposes. Why put the Christmas tree up? If the teacher intends to instruct her students on the history of this particular tradition, to introduce students to Christmas as a key holiday for those of the Christian faith, and if Christianity is just one of many religions examined by this teacher throughout the year, then she may be safe within legal and ethical boundaries. If, however, she intends to *celebrate* Christmas with her students, particularly to the exclusion of other religious holidays, then she has stepped beyond the appropriate role of the state into private, religious space.

Second, to what degree does putting up a Christmas tree advance or inhibit religion? Again, is the teacher using the tree as a means of celebration? And is Christmas the only holiday (and Christianity the only religion) celebrated in this classroom? Is one religion being advanced over others? Does putting up a Christmas tree inhibit the beliefs of atheist, Jewish, Muslim and other students, who often feel their own backgrounds are not the "correct" ones? If so, the teacher has, it seems, violated a constitutional principle. And finally, does putting up the Christmas tree avoid unnecessary entanglement with religion? Could the teacher just as easily explore Christmas and Christmas traditions with her students without erecting a tree in her classroom?

As you can see, each of these "tests" is merely a point of departure for evaluating the constitutionality of a given activity. The act of putting up the Christmas tree is neither "right" nor "wrong." It depends entirely on the intentions of the teacher who erected it and the ways it is used with students. The usefulness of the Lemon Tests continues to be contested among members of our Supreme Court. Some, like Justice O'Connor, have even offered alternatives. O'Connor has indicated that she is primarily concerned with whether a government action can be considered an "endorsement" of religion. In her words, an endorsement occurs when "a message to non-adherents that they are outsiders, not full members of the political community, and an accompanying message to adherents that they are insiders, favored members of the political community" is sent (for more on the "Town of Greece" case, visit: http://www.oyez.org/town-of-greece/). In this way, erecting a Christmas tree for the purpose of celebrating Christmas with fellow Christians would violate the Establishment Clause because it would signal to others their "insider" or "outsider" status. Though not hard and fast, the Lemon Tests and Justice O'Connor's more recent Endorsement Test provide a useful starting place for making sense of the legality of the decisions we make as teachers.

Free Exercise

The Free Exercise Clause says that all citizens have the right to practice their religion. No state or federal law can dictate one's private, religious practices. Of course, there are limits to what individuals can do in the name of religion. When one's private, religious beliefs infringe on the rights of others to "life, liberty, happiness" or their own right to religious freedom, the extent of our free exercise is checked. Like the Non-establishment Clause, the Free Exercise Clause has been tested time and again in our nation's highest court, and we have at our disposal some general guidelines for assessing whether a decision made by a school or teacher is in danger of violating students' right to believe what they choose to believe.

In 1963, the Court decided the *Sherbert v. Verner* case, in which Adell Sherbert, a member of the Seventh Day Adventist Church, was fired for refusing to work on Saturdays, her faith's Sabbath. When she filed for unemployment benefits, the state of South Carolina denied her request, rejecting her reason for refusing work. The Supreme Court ruled in her favor (seven to two), arguing that she had the right to practice her religion and refuse work on Saturdays. Since that time, the Court often considers two key questions when trying to assess whether the government has violated the Free Exercise Clause (commonly known as the "Sherbert Tests"). First, the Court asks whether the belief an individual claims has been violated is "sincere." Second, the Court asks whether the governmental act has caused an individual "substantial burden" (Haynes & Thomas, 2007).

Arguments about free exercise have included contestations against saying the Pledge of Allegiance, prayer at school-wide assemblies such as sporting events, and the wearing and posting of religious symbols in public school spaces. Let's revisit Christina, who at one point claimed that my requiring her to consider alternative viewpoints about good citizenship (and later controversial issues such as global warming), violated her right to free exercise of religion. When our university lawyers came to speak with us that spring, I asked specifically whether I had violated Christina's right to practice her religion by requiring her participation in an in-class discussion. Using these two Sherbert Tests, the lawyer explained that though Christina's belief may indeed be sincere (belief in one truth, one author of that truth), as a teacher I had likely not put any undue burden on her. First, I was teaching a social studies methods course, in which debate and discussion were reasonable topics and experiences. Second, the civic purpose of these activities (both for my students and for their students) was equally reasonable. I did not require that she believe what others believed or what I believed.

It is one thing to reflect on our aims and evaluate the civic intentions at the heart of our work. It is harder, however, to assess the burden felt by our students. Subtle pedagogical decisions may impact our students in ways that are hard for us to see. Students of mine have reported feeling ostracized by faculty and peers in her teacher education program. Luke reported that he often felt like an "outsider" in his classes. Laura said she felt like she was "crossing enemy lines" when she entered the education building and needed to steel herself for what was to come.

Then there was Rebecca. Not long after the close of our semester together, Rebecca visited my office. She asked to speak with me about the course, saying that she had finished the semester very troubled by some of the questions I had asked. She claimed to be undergoing a crisis of faith as a result of our time together. Like others before her, Rebecca spoke at length about her fear of what would happen if her parents, her friends, her boyfriend, her congregation knew she were questioning her faith. Rebecca's sense of place within her community and her sense of self as part of that community were intimately wrapped up in her theological certainty. Doubt—the very thing Griffin (1942/1996) insisted is most essential for democracy—was the thing she feared most. "My father would disown me," she said.

Other students speak more about their fear of not knowing who they would be if they began to question their deeply held beliefs. Matt, for instance, on the first day of class, introduced himself to his classmates this way: "I'm Matt, and I am through Christ." He couldn't imagine who he would be without his deeply rooted connection to the belief that defined him. And still others speak not of family or friends or even of their own identity, but fear of something much more grizzly that may fall upon them if they doubt: eternal damnation. Christina, for instance, believed that the very act of doubting meant the real possibility that she would spend eternity in hell.

For each of these students, the consequences of doubt—something they claim was brought on through participation in classroom discussion—involved a great deal more than epistemological discomfort or "cognitive dissonance." The perceived consequences were a personal loss of family, friends, community, a loss of identity, or potentially eternity with Satan. Students' allegiance to their community secured their part in something greater, but it also served to protect them from the worldliness outside. Acceptance of democracy, consideration of breaching this trust, was likened to sleeping with the enemy.

I do not take students' expressions lightly. They feel caught between the culture of their private worlds and the culture of their education programs—two cultures they find difficult to square up. To ascribe to the possibility of different truths feels like a betrayal of their faith and their faith community. Though I remain firm in my belief that deliberation and engagement with difference for the purposes of understanding and community-building are critical for a healthy democracy, I have become increasingly aware of the burden some students feel when I ask them to take up the work of democratic education with me. Particularly because they will one day be responsible for the education of other people's children—in public schools—I find the tension between their felt burden and the demands of democracy particularly acute. If they continue to think of open-mindedness as a burden, it is unlikely they will model it in their classrooms.

When faced with dilemmas like those described here, I return to the Establishment Clause, the Free Exercise Clause and the tests set forth by the Supreme

Court as guidelines. The Supreme Court clearly supports the civic mission of public schools. As a public school teacher, I am responsible for the civic education of young people. I find that having a clear vision of democratic education is helpful when I need to assess the ethics of my choices. Using the definition of democratic education set forth in Chapter 2, culled from democratic theory and the civic mission of schools, I can think more clearly about how each of my instructional choices moves that purpose forward. When religion intersects with my work as a teacher (through my own intention or not), how I navigate its intersection is best guided through a consideration of my democratic (civic) aims. Of course, things are not always clear. Often, even after careful reflection, there remain questions that leave me unsettled. I am today, however, much more confident in navigating these spaces in ways that balance my commitment to students and my commitment to democratic learning. In what follows, I share five principles that guide my practice.

Not Only Can We Teach about Religion, We Should

Not only are major religions the subject of many world civilization classes, but so too does religion figure into elementary social studies classrooms as students study people throughout time and around the world. Religion figures prominently in our own country's history and is central to many contemporary political debates. Including religion in our teaching is not only constitutional, but necessary if we are to help prepare students for participation in our diverse (and increasingly interdependent) world. "A person cannot be fully educated," wrote Justice Tom Clark in 1963, "without understanding the role of religion in history, culture and politics" (quoted in Haynes & Thomas, 2007, pvii).

What is important is that we are teaching *about* religion and doing so in a balanced way. What is not constitutional is preaching or proselytizing by teachers. Teachers are not to privilege or advocate one religion at the expense of others; nor are teachers to privilege religion over non-religion or vice versa. To the best of our ability, we ought to engage students in the study of diverse religious traditions for the purposes of expanding their understanding of the world around them and their place in it.

Where is the line between teaching about and leading students in religion? Teachers have asked me whether it is okay to introduce students to practices like yoga and meditation, to have various religious symbols in the classroom, to invite guest speakers to talk about their religious traditions and practices, to have a Bible in the classroom. Again the answer to these questions is: it depends. So long as our teaching is intended to introduce students to a range of religious practices for the purpose of broadening their understanding of themselves and others, then these are indeed appropriate methods. Including a range of texts (religious or about religion) in the classroom, bringing in symbols and pictures to help students gain first-hand and visual experience with religious traditions and practices, inviting guests to share their personal experiences with students . . . all of these approaches to the teaching of religion—if they are balanced and intended for civic purposes—are acceptable and can be powerful for students.

Students and Teachers Have a Right to Believe and Practice as They Choose . . . Even in Schools

At first glance, this guiding principle may seem in contradiction with the first. If we all have a right to believe and practice what we wish, why all the rules about a balanced approach? What's important here is that our right to practice and believe what we choose as individuals stops when it interferes with another's right to do the same. As teachers then, we must think carefully about the rights of our students and our responsibility for upholding them. The reach of particular religious practices and beliefs is limited to us as individuals and cannot be endorsed by the school or representatives of the school. Like our students, we have the right to believe what we choose and to adhere to our religion even while at work. As teachers we can wear religious symbols around our necks, pray over our own lunch, keep religious texts in our desk for study during a break. So long as we do not lead students in these activities—so long as they are activities we engage privately and for our own purposes—we do indeed have the right to free exercise. In the same vein, teachers should not be required to participate in religious activities led by others in the workplace that step outside of the civic mission of schools.

What if students ask about our religious beliefs? Can we share them? These are questions I get often from the pre-service teachers with whom I work. Again, I think the answer to these questions is: it depends. If we respond by sharing our beliefs and representing them as personal and one possible way to read the world (acknowledging the diversity of belief systems in our pluralistic society), then I imagine we are on safe ground. If we use this opportunity to try to persuade students to our particular belief system, that ground gets awfully slippery.

Students, of course, may also believe and practice as they wish and express their religious views in school. Christina had every right to call on her faith as a source for justifying her answer to my question about citizenship. As we'll see in Chapter 6, students' beliefs will surface in our classrooms in a variety of ways—overtly and subtly—as the lens through which they make sense of the content presented and the interactions they have with others. Making space to examine the role of beliefs in our sense-making about the world is an important part of a democratic education.

We Are Not Alone

As teachers, we often feel as if the dilemmas we face in teaching are ours to solve. The structure of schools places us alone in the classroom, imbued with the responsibility for educating the children before us . . . and at a rather fast pace.

There is little time to reflect or consult with peers, even less time to sit with students and puzzle together. These activities are critical, however, to engaging in ethical teaching. When religion and teaching intersect, it is rarely in predictable ways. Though I hope this chapter might serve as a compass for ethical practice, issues will surface that will fail to be easily resolved by the guidelines offered here. My own persistent fogginess was, after all, the impetus for this book.

So we must make time to think, to talk and to inquire. There are a few useful resources available for teachers interested in thinking deeply about the legal and ethical boundaries of their work. The First Amendment Center (whose resources I have drawn on heavily in the writing of this chapter) has provided me a great deal of clarity and been well received by the aspiring and practicing teachers with whom I work. They have two publications I highly recommend: *Finding common ground* (Haynes & Thomas, 2007) and *A teacher's guide to religion in the public schools* (Haynes, 2008). Peter Irons' book, *God on trial*, is another that I recommend for those interested in understanding the history of the issues introduced here. The National Council for the Social Studies has position statements about the role of religion in democratic education and the standards serve as a useful guide for knowing when to intentionally include religion in our teaching (see http://www.ncss.org).

As I've shared in the preceding chapters, I have often called on my colleagues to help me think through the dilemmas I face when religion makes an unexpected appearance in my classroom. Sometimes, they have lessons to share from having acted in the face of similar challenges in the past. Sometimes they are just as puzzled as I am. Nonetheless, I have appreciated the opportunities we've had to talk and think together. Perhaps our best partners in navigating the ethical spaces of schools, however, are our students. My students have been my very best teachers. If we truly want to understand students' experience of our pedagogy, we must create safe places for them to express themselves. If they do feel a burden as a result of pedagogical choices we've made, we must ask. They will only come to understand the reasons for the burden we ask them to carry if we share in turn. Keeping religion off the table denies all of us the opportunity to think about the complex roles it plays in our world.

It's Important to Step Outside Once in a While

Listening to our students is critical. It is one means of getting outside of our own heads long enough to consider the perspectives of those most impacted by the choices we make in schools. It may also be the most powerful way to see what we cannot see for ourselves. Most U.S. educators self-identify as Christian, and so some of the overtly religious practices of schools feel "normal," as we'll see in the next chapter. But it only takes a moment to turn these "normal" practices on their end, to look at them through different eyes, to begin to see the ways they can make students feel pressed upon to either conform or feel like outsiders.

One thing I have sometimes asked myself is whether I would be comfortable if another teacher—with a different set of religious understandings than my own—was teaching in the ways that I am. When I do this, I am forced to think carefully about what I have said and how I have responded to students' words and actions in the classroom. If my own children were in a classroom like mine, with a teacher who believed differently than I believe, would I be comfortable with her doing as I do?

Concluding Thoughts

To know what is legal we can look to the court for precedent. To know what is ethical is a bit trickier. Farhi ultimately attended music class when the teacher convinced his parents that they were merely studying different genres of music and learning to read music, not using it for celebratory purposes or religious observance. Shara's dad eventually acquiesced to have her tested for a learning disability when she reached fifth grade. It seems though that he could have held out as long as he wished. He grew tired, I think, of our pestering. Harry Potter? Not banned. But the issue did go all the way to the superintendent's office before a final decision was made. In the meantime, we were all asked to refrain from reading the text aloud. The preschool teacher kept doing yoga, among other approaches to "Movement" in her classroom. The parent had her daughter reassigned and life went on.

These anecdotes, though they may seem random, dot my journey as a teacher in fairly consistent fashion. Rarely has an issue over religion in the classroom been as clear cut as, say, should I or should I not lead my students in prayer? Much more often religion intersects with my work in subtle and complicated ways. I have sometimes wished there was a court in my classroom closet where I could turn for help—especially when my instructional decision-making leads to students feeling a burden that I didn't intend. Sadly, such a miniature court does not exist. The best we have is to act with care and mindfulness, humility and caution. It's in this place, it seems to me, that ethical practice has the greatest chance to grow.

References

Griffin, A.F. (1942/1996). Teaching in democratic and authoritarian states. In W.C. Parker, *Educating the democratic mind* (pp. 79–93). New York, NY: SUNY Press.

Haynes, C.C. (2008). *A teacher's guide to religion in the public schools.* Nashville, TN: The First Amendment Center.

Haynes, C.C., & Thomas, O. (2007). *Finding common ground: A first amendment guide to religion in public schools.* Nashville, TN: The First Amendment Center.

Irons, P. (2007). *God on trial: Dispatches from America's religious battlefields.* New York, NY: Penguin Group.

Madison, J. (1785). *Memorial and remonstrance.* Retrieved from: http://www.law.gmu.edu/assets/files/academics/founders/Madison'sMemorial.pdf

4

THE NOT-SO-HIDDEN CURRICULUM OF RELIGION IN PUBLIC SCHOOLS

Guiding Questions:

In what ways is religion present in our public schools?
How is it that religion persists there?
What are the consequences for democratic living and learning?

"We're all Christian here." So said Lynn, self-designated room-mom for my daughter's second-grade class. As a new parent at the school, I had signed up to help with class celebrations, thinking it would give me an opportunity to spend time with my daughter and her new friends. It was mid-November, and the "Winter Party Committee" was meeting over coffee at the local Panera. Six moms, Lynn and myself included, sat around two tables we had pulled together for the purpose of brainstorming ideas for the upcoming party. While sipping my coffee and munching my bagel, I scanned the mounds of material scattered across the table tops: elf stickers, craft ideas cut from magazines for making advent calendars and Christmas cards, articles describing fun holiday games like Pin-the-Nose-on-Rudolph-the-Reindeer, puzzles and coloring sheets filled with decorated trees, stars, Santa Claus, candy canes and stockings . . . As the group discussed different "fun stations" they could hold during the hour-long celebration, I wondered whether I was the only one at the table who felt this was shaping up to be more of a Christmas party than a Winter one. So, as I've been known to do, I opened my mouth to ask the question others wished I wouldn't. The friendly chatter came to an abrupt halt as the other four women looked to Lynn, who lifted her eyes from her pile of magazine clippings, looked me directly in the eye, and with no small amount of disdain, offered the response that started this paragraph: "We're all Christian here."

Hmmm, I thought. Maybe. Though I'd only lived in the area for a little over a year, I had met many neighbors, community members and colleagues at the university where I worked, a rather surprising number of whom were self-declared agnostics, atheists, Orthodox and Reform Jews. Was it true that every family in my daughter's class was Christian? Possible, I thought. Possible, but not likely. I spoke again, this time offering, "Even so. I mean, even if we're all Christian here, might that be a good reason to introduce our children to traditions other than ones they know? What better time than during a Winter holiday party to share different types of celebrations with our kids?" Silence again as Lynn looked at the other women around the table, rolled her eyes, and said, "Sure, why not. Why don't you pick one and you can run a station of your own."

Such is the consequence bestowed on someone who opens her mouth when she should know better to keep it closed. So there I was, tasked with designing a station of my very own for the Winter-Holiday-Christmas party. Though Hanukkah is not a major holiday in the Jewish faith, it is one celebrated by a number of my friends, one with which I was at least a little familiar. Hanukkah it would be. Next was to come up with something "fun" to have the students do. I managed to find a few books at the library. Locating dreidels and Hanukkah gelt was a much greater challenge than I anticipated, but eventually I found a party supplier online who shipped the necessary items directly to my home.

December 17, I arrived, shopping bags in hand, ready to set up my station. One of the other committee moms pointed to an empty table set up in the corner of the room. "That one's yours," she said. Fabulous. Tucked away in the corner, a pressing reminder of the marginalization of anything non-Christian in this "We're all Christian here" classroom. I would be part of the celebration, however, so that was something.

Once set up, the kids returned from music class, were assigned to groups and invited to start their rotation around the room. Each child would visit each fun station for approximately 10 minutes: Christmas cookie decorating, Christmas card making, Pin-the-Nose-on-Rudolph-the-Reindeer, Christmas puzzle sheets and . . . Hanukkah! Let the festivities begin! My first group of seven-year-olds arrived at the Hanukkah table looking puzzled. "What is this?" a little girl named Eva asked with some measure of disappointment. "I thought this was a Christmas party."

"I thought it would be nice to talk about another holiday people celebrate this time of year," I replied. "We're going to learn a little about Hanukkah and play a game. Do you know anything about Hanukkah?"

"Yeah," she answered. "I know it's not as important as Christmas."

Yikes. *Okay, so now what?* I thought. "It's important to some people," I said to her.

To which she replied, "Well, it's not important to me."

***

This is a true story. So too is the story that follows, in which a parent I had never met before stopped by my "fun station" to say she thought it was very nice of me to bring my family's unique customs into the classroom, an exchange that left me feeling strangely othered. I'm not sure what bothered me more—the fact that she assumed only a Jewish person would have any reason to talk about Hanukkah or the fact that she talked to me like I was visiting from outer space. Then there was my daughter, who begged—pleaded—for me to try to play nicer with the other moms in the future and just BE NORMAL.

The word *normal* was often to be confused with Christian in this context, I would come to learn over time. Maya, my Jewish colleague and friend's five-year-old daughter, used the same word when she asked her parents if she could stay home from school the day before winter break. Santa Claus was coming and if her parents wouldn't let her sit on his lap like the rest of the kids, she didn't want to go. "Why can't we just be NORMAL?" she implored. Though I had been mistakenly identified as "other" at the classroom party because of my bold act of discussing Hanukkah at an otherwise very-merry-Christmas party, little Maya is indeed Jewish. Other. And the public school she attended had no bones about making her feel *ab*normal.

These examples of explicit religious practice in our nation's public schools may surprise you. Maybe they don't. Interestingly, they're fairly common. Erik Eckholm, in a 2011 *New York Times* article, argues that "especially in the rural South, open prayer and Christian symbols have never really disappeared from schools, with what legal advocates call brazen violations of the law coming to light many times each year." He goes on to unravel a list of "violations" including a middle school assembly in South Carolina where a rapper was invited to share his religious conversion experience with students, a teacher preaching over a bullhorn as students arrived at school in Florida, and teacher-led Bible studies in Tennessee. In schools across the country—up and down the eastern seaboard, in the Midwest and in California—I have seen Christmas tree after Christmas tree in halls and classrooms, sat through pageants and concerts where children performed Christmas songs for an adoring audience of parents, teachers and friends. I have watched classrooms full of children, led by their teachers, say grace before snack was served. In a school my daughters attended there was held an annual school-wide *Polar Express* Day, where each class of children was given a 30-minute period to visit the library, listen to the popular Chris Van Allsburg text read aloud, sip on hot cocoa and have a bell strung around their necks as a volunteer parent whispers "Believe" in their ears. In Santa, that is. Believe in Santa. (Troubling not only for non-Christian students, but also for those children whose families can't afford to have Santa visit.) This event is so popular, in fact, that each December the school holds an Alumni *Polar Express* Night, when former students come back to relive this magical experience from their youth.

These practices are common, yes. But not likely constitutional. As discussed in Chapter 3, the Supreme Court has ruled it *un*constitutional for a teacher or school to proselytize or privilege one religion over others. As a nation, we profess that we have effectively separated church and state, and yet our schools remain a contested space where public and private—religious—interests swirl about, vying for airtime. Despite our separatist claim, religion persists in the education of our children, and we are not altogether sure we want it to go away. One doesn't have to go far to find a raft of publications—articles, books, documentaries—addressing the relationship between religion and schooling. We continue to debate whether prayer has a place in schools, the inclusion of the phrase "under God" in the pledge of allegiance, the use of religious symbols in school ceremonies . . . Though our courts have ruled time and again against the privileging of one faith over others in public spaces, we continue to believe that our schools are up for grabs. Why?

Present and Persistent

What contributes to our belief that religion—particularly of a Judeo-Christian stripe—ought to have a place in our public schools? In what follows, I unpack three prevailing arguments found in scholarly and mainstream conversations about the persistence of religion in schools, and what I believe to be their implications for democratic education.

Argument #1: Schools Are (and Ought to Be) a Reflection of the Communities in Which They Sit

Schools are public spaces where students from surrounding neighborhoods and communities gather daily. As we would expect, students bring with them their own cultural and familial experiences and understandings into the classroom. To the degree that those experiences and understandings are welcomed and affirmed in the life of the school itself, they become part of the discursive and institutional space students inhabit. For many people, the fact that schools reflect their local communities feels natural and right. Parents, in particular, often feel as if the school their child attends should be a place that reflects their commitments and values—especially if those parents are active—giving time or money—to the school. Among white middle-class parents, in particular, there is typically a shared expectation that "good" parents participate in the education of their children by engaging in the activities of the school, by being present, speaking out and working to shape the experiences their children have there (Lareau, 2000; Valenzuela, 1999). With parents as educative partners, however, the public space of schools becomes infused with private interests, and often the interests of those with the most social capital reign. This makes it difficult to parse out what is good for some and what may be in the interest of all.

It is striking, in fact, the fervor with which some parents speak out about the role of schools to extend the education of the family and preserve a particular cultural heritage. My good friend, Agnes, upon returning to her local elementary school after a two-year stint abroad, was appalled to learn that they were no longer holding a Christmas concert in December. "What is going on in this place?!" she demanded, "Just because a couple of non-Christian students enroll, the whole school has to give up its right to celebrate Christmas?" Like Lynn, who claimed that "we're all Christian here'" Agnes seemed to believe that there was a cultural (religious) majority at her neighborhood school and that that majority should be able to expect—indeed had a *right* to expect—that the school would embody the traditions and values that majority held dear. I can only imagine the outcry that would follow if my daughter's school decided not to hold *Polar Express* Day. Grandparents of currently enrolled students have such fond memories of this event, it is woven into the community's collective memory—the school having essentially become responsible for preserving it.

I often hear people argue that if a school was more diverse, it would make sense for teachers to celebrate different holidays, teach different traditions. Again, this argument reflects the shared belief that a neighborhood school should embody and reflect the religious and cultural identity of the larger community. But does this mean that when the larger community is fairly homogeneous, students do not (and ought not to) have opportunities to learn about difference? And what of schools where administrators have decided that there should be no discussion of religion at all? The school where I began my career took this stance—we were so diverse, there was no way to do justice to each student's cultural heritage, so we would have no class or school-wide celebrations. Period.

Both instances—preserving one particular cultural or religious narrative or intentionally ignoring all cultural or religious narratives—are unconstitutional practices and contend with the aims of democratic education. As the opening vignette reveals, affirming children's identity can be good, but can also be dangerously othering and disruptive to the goals of growing appreciation for diverse ways of being. Students and families of non-Christian religious and non-religious backgrounds are consistently reminded of their otherness. Christian students, too, learn powerful lessons from the pervasiveness of Christianity they experience in schools. Even in classrooms where teachers make an occasional effort to read a book on Eid-al-Fitr or sing a dreidel song, students are quick to interpret the relative importance of differing religious and cultural practices. Democratic principles of tolerance, equity and a common good are undermined when such imbalances go unchecked.

Argument #2: Teachers Are Moral Educators Responsible for Raising "Good" Kids

In my own research about teaching and religion, I have come to understand that for many educators, particularly elementary school teachers, moral education plays a primary role in the work they ascribe themselves. Many elementary teachers go into teaching because they "love kids" and because they hope to serve as surrogate parents for their students. For some, being a teacher is a wonderful training ground for becoming parents themselves. These aspiring and practicing teachers see themselves as tasked with raising other people's children, responsible for their social, emotional and moral development as well as their academic and intellectual growth. In a recent research study, kindergarten teacher Sarah, said:

> My students are my babies, and I need to mother them, and I need to take care of them and they need to feel safe. And so I work with them and I love them and I hug them and give them kisses on the top of their heads and hold their hands.
>
> (Interview, April 6)

Here, Sarah proudly assumes the role of mother to her students. She talks of loving them, giving kisses, holding their hands; all things Sarah, the mother, does. Perhaps unintentionally, however, she projects her own ideas of mothering (and of caring) onto students whose cultures and familial experiences may be very different from her own.

As moral authorities in the classroom, teachers draw on what they know and hold to be true, they draw on their experience of child rearing—either their own experiences as children or their experiences as parents themselves. And often, their notions of child rearing are laden with religious understandings. Because the image of teacher as mother is so common, and because schools are often expected to reflect the dominant culture of the communities in which they sit (a culture shared by most teachers), teachers may not feel compelled to stop and think about the cultural incongruencies that exist between themselves and their students. Take, for instance, my older daughter's second-grade teacher who explained that she led her students in saying grace each day in order to impart important lessons about being grateful for what we have. But grateful to whom? This seemingly innocent moral education lesson, which acknowledged God as giver of all things good, claims a privileged space for monotheistic religious belief.

When teachers do acknowledge differences that exist between their students and themselves, they often characterize those differences as problematic or inconvenient. A recent pre-service teacher shared with me a story about a Jehovah's Witness child in her class who "was such a problem" because she could not participate in class or school-wide celebrations. Each time the class wanted to hold a birthday party, for instance, she had to find something else for the child to do, an added chore and inconvenience. The teacher expressed her frustration, but also pity for the student, who she felt had been routinely denied the opportunity to have her own birthday celebrated. Similarly, Islamic children tend to be sent to the library or other "holding" spaces during the month-long observation of Ramadan, when they must fast. Students who miss school for Jewish holidays require additional time from the teacher to make up what was missed, and are often seen as adding to a teacher's workload.

Not only does students' religion present a problem for the larger group and the teacher, but because the experiences of students and families are scripted differently than those of the teachers with whom they work, they are often deemed lacking in important ways (Valdes, 2001, 1996; Valenzuela, 1999). Ladson-Billings (1994) writes about assimilationist teaching that invalidates culture and experience that stands outside the dominant frame. Caring that is assimilationist, or that imposes one's cultural norms on another, fails to achieve mutuality, a key element of democratic living. Interestingly, deficit and mothering discourses are often coupled in teacher talk. Principal Dawn said in a recent study, "They're often mothers to these kids or at least second mothers because they're teaching them socialization skills, survival skills and things that in many homes we take for granted but they don't have." That Dawn couples mothering with deficit talk about students' lives outside of school suggests that mothering of this kind is particularly necessary in a setting such as this one where students have such exceptional needs.

Often, the deficiencies identified in students have to do with teachers' assessment of their religiosity. Christina, as a student teacher, for example, shared that working with non-Christians posed a unique challenge for her. She loved them, of course, but felt sad for children who had not established a relationship with Jesus Christ. As a way to correct for this deficiency, she described engaging in "undercover work for Jesus" through which she prayed for the children, their families and their communities—all of which she deemed lacking. It is hard to know how this belief about students' spiritual deficiencies plays out in Christina's daily practice, if at all. It is troubling, however, that she starts from the premise that her students are deficient in what she feels is such an important way. Interestingly, in the field of English-language teaching, recent work has explored the rising numbers of evangelical Christian educators who claim to see second-language teaching as missionary work. Such framing informs both their interactions with and perceptions of students. One participant says, "It does *sicken* me sometimes to the core to think that Phuong, you know my Vietnamese girl I love so much, in the way that I believe will spend eternity in hell if she does not make the right decision about Jesus. But I cannot make that for her" (Varghese & Johnston, 2007, p. 21).

The power of deficit and mothering discourses rests in their ability to affirm one another. A mothering discourse precludes the need to listen closely to students as it privatizes the classroom space and puts the teacher in the position of moral authority over students. Deficit talk about students reifies notions of teaching as mothering by presupposing that students lack sufficient parenting at home. In the midst of these powerful discourses about students' needs and the responsibility of the teacher to meet those needs, then, teachers often do not feel compelled to listen with humility and caution. As a result, democratic living is stunted.

Argument #3: Christianity Has Become Secularized

Others argue that Christianity, and in particular holidays such as Christmas and Easter, have been so secularized that they cease to be religious in nature, so why not welcome them in schools? One could put up a Christmas tree without believing in the story of Jesus, for instance. Students in my teacher education courses have argued that Easter doesn't even resemble Easter when talk is of eggs and bunny rabbits. That if we do not tell the story of Christ's crucifixion and resurrection, do not explain the significance of the cross as symbol of ultimate sacrifice and salvation, we are not honoring the Easter story at all. These students have no problem with the idea of Easter egg hunts, egg dying activities, or baskets full of candy in public schools.

Despite the fading of the Biblical stories attached to Christmas and Easter, the shared celebration of these holidays presses on the idea that the "we" of the school, as a community, share a set of common cultural understandings grounded in a particular religious tradition. If I do not celebrate Christmas, but my school does, whether we mention Jesus or not, the explicit inclusion of this particular holiday over others sends powerful messages about a privileged or normalized way of being in the world. If I do celebrate Christmas, whether I am deeply religious or not, the fact that my school reinforces this celebration at the exclusion of others sends me equally compelling messages about the rightness, the pervasiveness and the dominance of my cultural heritage.

That schools have subsumed Judeo-Christian traditions, language, rhythms and epistemologies is explained by a walk through history, back to the common school movement and its roots in Protestantism and European monastic traditions, as I will discuss later in this chapter. These practices have been taken up by our public institutions and thus, in a sense, have been "secularized." Yet the very fact that these remnants of the past echo so faintly—indeed *because* they are largely invisible and understood as secular—points to the very issue I am raising. How is it that the religious and the secular have become so entwined that we can hardly tell them apart? If indeed Christian and secular become one—conflated—even in tertiary or superficial ways, what are the implications for democratic living and learning in schools?

These three arguments, commonly offered in scholarly and popular conversations and adopted by teachers and parents themselves, work together to bolster the overt presence of religion in schools. We generally believe that schools should reflect the communities in which they sit, meaning that if "we are all Christian here," we may legitimately live out our Christian identities in school. We typically agree that the Christianity that shows up in schools has been secularized, so are able to get over any claim that religion and schooling are overly entwined. And because we share in the belief that teachers ought to help raise good children, we allow them to assume responsibility for imparting moral lessons of their choosing, something we feel generally comfortable doing so long as the teacher shares our values. Prevailing narratives about teaching, about schooling and about religion work together to justify our unwillingness to relinquish a Judeo-Christian hold on our nation's public schools.

"But wait!" you say. "We don't do this in MY school!" Of course there are many examples of teachers and schools making every effort to know and engage their students democratically, resisting teaching explicit religious lessons. But lest we too quickly pat ourselves on the back for refusing to engage in such explicit religious practices, we must—for a moment—take a closer look at the ways religion may be much more subtly present in schools. The "hidden" curriculum of religion in schools is perhaps even more problematic than the overt examples discussed above. The power of this curriculum lies in its invisibility, its seeming neutrality, and its taken-for-grantedness.

Remnants of the Past

From the early days of English colonization in North America, education was understood as a means of developing and maintaining local religious customs. Colonies such as Massachusetts required each township to appoint teachers who would be responsible for the development of children's literacy, so that they would be able to read the Bible—"It being one chief project of that old deluder, Satan, to keep men from the knowledge of the Scriptures" (Fraser, 1999, p. 10). Later, the common school movement of the 19th Century developed, in part, as a response to the growing presence of European immigrants of diverse religious backgrounds, particularly Roman Catholics (Carper & Hunt, 2007). Although schools moved away from the denominational specificity of the community-based parochial schools of the colonial era, they nonetheless emphasized practices (including Bible reading) consistent with non-denominational Protestantism. The influence of these religious origins, although still pervasive, has become as invisible as the foundation on which the schoolhouse is built.

Organization of Time

One way in which Christianity continues to shape schools is in the structure of the school day, week and year. Although to many people there seems to be nothing overtly religious about the school day, scholars have argued that our collective quest for organization and control, which manifests in the cellularization of students' lives in school, has its origins in monastic Europe (Burke & Segall, 2011; Foucault, 1977). Jenks (2001) argues that the strict organizational structures we find in today's schools (students in rows, 50-minute classes, compartmentalized subject matter, etc.) are imbued with surveillance and disciplinary aims. The goal, ultimately, is, and has always been, disciplined bodies and submission to external authority.

The school day not only has traces of monastic rhythms and patterns in its structure, but also reflects larger cultural practices of Judeo-Christian communities. For Muslim students—who are required to pray at particular times of day— the daily schedule is clearly a vestige of schools' Christian origins. So too is the weekly schedule: both required attendance and extra-curricular activities accord well with the pattern of religious observation for most Christians. Some Jewish students, on the other hand, must miss athletic or other activities on Friday evenings and Saturday, while Muslim students often must choose between attending school or mosque on Friday afternoons. The school year, meanwhile, obviously is structured around Christian holidays, with major vacations occurring around both Easter and Christmas, while holidays of other traditions go unacknowledged—forcing some Jewish students to miss graduation because of Shavuot, for example, or Muslim students to attend school while weak or tired during the fasting of Ramadan.

Conceptions of Goodness

The common school movement of the 19th Century emphasized a non-denominational Protestant morality in place of specific religious instruction. This generalized approach to religion, or moral education, offered a starting point for a set of shared American values: a model citizen would demonstrate respect for authority, responsibility for his own work, self-control, persistence, patriotism and loyalty—even if that loyalty was now to a more general God and country than in the previous century (Pulliam & Van Patten, 1995). As Fraser (1999) notes, "The vast majority of nineteenth-century American Protestants could happily and safely assign the larger enterprise of building and transmitting an American culture to the common schools, confident that the students were being enculturated in a religious world that was comfortably familiar" (p. 43).

A visit to a local elementary school reveals just how closely tied these values are to popular and contemporary notions of what it means to be American. Last October, during one elementary school's school-wide assembly, the principal proudly announced that she had "caught" many students demonstrating good citizenship in the first few days of school. She lauded individuals and groups for "respecting their teachers, following directions, using their time wisely, and exhibiting self-control." After leading the entire student body in a recitation of the Pledge of Allegiance, she reminded parents of their shared responsibility to raise "good little citizens." Although many people would perceive values such as time management and self-control as general American ones, they are rooted in the Puritan ideals celebrated in the *New England Primer* and the later pan-Protestant values reflected in the *McGuffey Readers*. This "common morality," institutionalized over the past three centuries and more, fails to recognize the ever-growing diversity of the nation's students, many of whom come from backgrounds that differ in their understandings and expressions of values such as timeliness, respect for elders and the importance of individual self-direction (cf. Pulliam & Van Patten, 1995). That disparities in expectations across cultural and class groups lead to consistent gaps in academic achievement is well documented, and yet this seems to have little impact on the daily practice of most classrooms.

Language

Judeo-Christian understandings pervade our language as well. Words like dean, rector, mission statement, convocation, office, discipline—all have their roots in Christianity, leading to "a normalized and not-so-silent authoritative religious discourse" (Burke & Segall, 2011, p. 644). The word "dean," though it commonly refers to the head of a school or college, has ecclesiastical roots. The term also means "the head of the chapter of a cathedral" (dictionary.com). Every school and district has a "mission" statement, yet another term with religious origins: "a group of people sent by a religious body, especially a Christian church, to a foreign country to do religious and social work." Even words like office and discipline are born of a close relationship with Christianity: "office: a ceremony or service, prescribed by ecclesiastical authorities"; "discipline: the laws governing members of a Church."

The religious origins of these words (and many others) may not be widely known. I don't imagine that school faculty members consider the Christian meaning of the word "office" or "discipline" when they are discussing school affairs. As Burke and Segall (2011) argue, however,

> [w]hether or how the Christian roots of the above terms and objects matters to those working within educational settings might vary, but the idea that we continuously convey religious sediments in our daily use of these terms and the ideological and pedagogical positions those invite for ourselves and our students, including those who are not Christian, ought to require some pause in institutions that tend to define themselves as secular and who have made various efforts to otherwise ensure the separation of religion and education and regularly insist, based on established court decisions, on refraining from promoting religion. What the use of such terms demonstrates is that, while overt promotion of religious belief might indeed be avoided, implicit messages read critically, regarding religion—and Christianity in particular—seem ever present.

(p. 643)

Relationship to Knowledge and Knowing

Yet another example of a hidden curriculum with roots in Christianity is the epistemology of text and our prevailing relationship to knowledge in the public school. Our over-reliance on the textbook as the source of knowledge in the classroom points to a shared understanding about singular truths and our belief that authority for knowledge construction lies with experts rather than with students themselves. Segall and Burke (2013) argue, "Seeing textbooks, or the Bible, as canonical, presents a closed sense of the world and of what readings of it might entail" (p. 317). Despite decades of research on the power of active learning strategies, inquiry and problem-based learning, students are still largely asked to memorize and recite discrete bits of knowledge imparted by an external authority—textbook or teacher. This practice—"a form of testament rather than of education" (Segall & Burke, 2013, p. 317)—is historically rooted in notions of education that privilege obedience to a particular moral code and set of beliefs. Recent comments by the Republican Party of Texas suggest that sticking close to a dissemination model of teaching that adheres to singular truths continues to be a priority:

> We oppose the teaching of Higher Order Thinking Skills (HOTS) (values clarification), critical thinking skills and similar programs that are simply a relabeling of Outcome-Based Education (OBE) (mastery learning) which focus on behavior modification and have the purpose of challenging the student's fixed beliefs and undermining parental authority.
> (Republican Party of Texas, 2012, quoted in Whittaker, 2012)

Valerie Strauss, in her 2012 *Washington Post* article, adds: "[The Party] opposes, among other things, early childhood education, sex education, and multicultural education, but supports 'school subjects with emphasis on the Judeo-Christian principles upon which America was founded.'" So while, for some, the overwhelming affinity for prescription, transmission and conformity are merely relics of an earlier time, unenlightened by more recent scholarship on teaching and learning, for others it is still the preferred way of doing school.

Such methods of teaching, however, not only fail to acknowledge decades of research on how students learn, but also hinder opportunities for democratic education. Or maybe that's the point? Here we run up against another skeleton in our closet: education as a means of assimilation. Schools have historically served as "a powerful force in attempting to detach outsiders and the naïve from their culturally 'unacceptable' and 'alien' customs and teaching them appropriate 'American ways' to think and behave" (VanSledright, 2008, pp. 110–111).

In our efforts to assimilate others, however, "American nationalism has also," as Gerstle (1997) observes,

> derived its power from its ability to exclude and denigrate others. Within our borders, Indians, blacks, Tories, Irish Catholics, Asians, southern and

eastern Europeans, Communists, anarchists, homosexuals, and even monopolists and "plutocrats" have served as "others" against whom "we" have defined our Americanness.

(p. 577)

Such sentiment is reflected in the 2012 Texas GOP platform:

American Identity Patriotism and Loyalty—We believe the current teaching of a multicultural curriculum is divisive. We favor strengthening our common American identity and loyalty instead of political correctness that nurtures alienation among racial and ethnic groups. Students should pledge allegiance to the American and Texas flags daily to instill patriotism.

(Strauss, 2012)

Of course, politics, religion and education are entangled. They have long been and will continue to be. But we must not be afraid to ask the difficult questions: who is best served by the current order? Whose identity is "common"? Loyalty and allegiance to what? Regardless of one's political standing, we must always ask about the consequences of our decisions, not just for ourselves, but for society as a whole. If majority rules in the case of a moral code taught in our nation's public schools, democracy is threatened. As Parker (2003) argues:

In an interesting way—some find it paradoxical—liberty and democracy rely on diversity; they need it . . . a multiplicity of minority factions keeps any one from tyrannizing the whole of society. Minority factions, therefore, are not a problem in a democracy; rather, the majority is the problem.

(p. 28)

That we continue to debate the role of religion in schools is the sign of a healthy democracy. It is when we stop asking, instead justifying religion's presence as neutral, secular or invisible, that we have ceased to take seriously our responsibility for educating our students for democracy. A failure on our part, as educators, to acknowledge the subtle and not-so-subtle ways politics and religion shape the experiences available to students in our public schools, is the same as choosing to accept the status quo unconditionally. And the status quo for most students means being kept from the process of knowledge construction (as participants rather than recipients) and discouraged from asking critical questions of truths established by others. Education in this vein is passive; students are consumers. If indeed, as Parker (2003) argues, "educators are the primary stewards of democracy," then we must do better.

Dilemmas for Democratic Education: Paying Attention

It would be rare these days to find a teacher preaching from the King James Bible in a public school classroom. Christianity, however, continues to serve as the public school's moral compass and normative frame within which institutional and pedagogical decisions are made. Those who argue that religion is absent in public schools fail to recognize this reality. The invisibility of religion, its taken-for-grantedness, ought not to be mistaken for absence. Rather, we must interrogate the ways religion shapes what goes on in public schools and strive for a more critical, comprehensive and equitable approach.

As laid out in the opening chapters of this book, democratic education involves openness, persistent inquiry and a desire to transcend the private spaces we inhabit to engage in political decision-making that strives for a common good. If, as Barber (2003) argues, democracy is always in the making, if our common good is always provisional—then we must be in the business of asking ourselves what it is we take for granted, why, and what that taken-for-grantedness means for students in schools.

The consequences of leaving religion's presence in schools unexamined are steep. Students are likely to leave with severe misunderstandings about religions and about religion in general, intolerant of different ideas and people who hold them, limited in their willingness or ability to talk across difference, failing to recognize the ways their own beliefs shape their understandings. Teachers are likely to continue working in fear of letting religion "slip in" to their teaching—all the while misunderstanding their roles as educators, anxious about parent or administrator backlash, and equally unaware of how their own beliefs inform their work. Such outcomes would be unfortunate not only for the students and teachers themselves, but for the communities of which they are a part.

What might such a commitment to paying attention involve? To begin with, responsible teaching, I would argue, must include critical reflection on our beliefs as they inform our aims and practices. We must seek out professional development that helps to clarify the legal and ethical boundaries of our work with students, deepen our knowledge of religious diversity, and enhance our repertoire of pedagogical methods for engaging students in the study of religion. Students must be encouraged to consider the prevailing narratives at work in their own sense-making, to move beyond generalizations about "others," and to make connections between the content and the world around them.

Likewise, the curriculum must reflect ongoing research on how to include deliberation of controversial political issues, so as to provide students ample opportunity for exploring relevant, complex issues and developing comfort with talking across difference. The curriculum ought to include various perspectives on the past (not only through a Judeo-Christian lens) in order to more fully represent historical events. Administrators and school faculty must take the time to rethink the prevailing practices and values at work in their school buildings, and to ask critical questions about their limits and consequences. And finally, teachers and scholars alike must actively work to disrupt inequitable practices and discourses that perpetuate them. Popular notions of an invisible line between schools and religion, or of the importance of striving for neutrality in teaching, the conflation of teaching and preaching—all of these are discourses in need of undoing. Paying attention to them is the first step.

References

Barber, B. (2003). *Strong democracy: Participatory politics for a new age*. Berkeley, CA: University of California Press.

Burke, K.J., & Segall, A. (2011) Christianity and its legacy in education. *Journal of Curriculum Studies, 43*(5), 631–658.

Carper, J.C., & Hunt, T.C. (2007). *The dissenting tradition in American education*. New York: Peter Lang.

Eckholm, E. (2011). Battling anew over the place of religion in public schools. *New York Times*, December 28, p. 10.

Foucault, M. (1977). *Language, counter-memory, practice*. Translated by D. Bouchard and S. Simon. Ithaca, NY: Cornell University Press.

Fraser, J.W. (1999). *Between church and state: Religion and public education in a multicultural America*. New York: St. Martin's Griffin.

Gerstle, G. (1997). The power of nations. *Journal of American History, 84*, 576–580.

Jenks, C. (2001). The pacing and timing of children's bodies. In V. Hultqvist and V. Dahlberg (Eds.), *Governing the child in the new millennium* (pp. 68–84). London: Routledge Falmer.

Ladson-Billings, G. (1994). *The dreamkeepers: Successful teachers of African-American children*. San Francisco, CA: Jossey Bass.

Lareau, A. (2000). *Home advantage: Social class and parental intervention in elementary education* (2nd ed.). Lanham, MD: Rowman & Littlefield Publishers, Inc.

Parker, W.C. (2003). *Teaching democracy: Unity and diversity in public life*. New York, NY: Teachers College Press.

Pulliam, J.D., & Van Patten, J. (1995). *History of education in America* (6th ed.). Englewood Cliffs, NJ: Merrill.

Segall, A., & Burke, K. (2013). Reading the Bible as a pedagogical text: Testing, testament, and some postmodern considerations about religion/the Bible in contemporary education. *Curriculum Inquiry 43*(3), 305–330.

Strauss, V. (2012). Texas GOP rejects 'critical thinking' skills. Really. *The Washington Post*, July 9.

Valdes, G. (1996). *Con respeto: Bridging the distances between culturally diverse families and schools*. New York, NY: Teachers College Press.

Valdes, G. (2001). *Learning and not learning English: Latino students in American schools*. New York, NY: Teachers College Press.

Valenzuela, A. (1999). *Subtractive schooling: U.S.-Mexican youth and the politics of caring*. Albany, New York: SUNY Press.

VanSledright, B.A. (2008). Narratives of nation-state, historical knowledge, and school history education. *Review of Educational Research, 32*, 109–146.

Varghese, M.M., & Johnston, B. (2007). Evangelical Christians and English language teaching. *TESOL Quarterly*, *41*(1), 5–31.

Whittaker, R. (2012). GOP opposes critical thinking. *Austin Chronicle*, June 27. Retrieved from: http://www.austinchronicle.com/daily/news/2012-06-27/gop-opposes-critical-thinking/

5

UNPACKING NARRATIVES OF CALLING AND PURPOSE IN TEACHING

Kimberly Logan

Guiding Questions:

How do teachers' religious understandings shape their purposes and practice as teachers?
What might get in the way?
How might we encourage spaces for self-reflexivity, understanding and dialogue?

> Consciously, we teach what we know; unconsciously we teach who we are.
> (Hamachek, 1999, p. 209)

My interest in teachers' religious understandings evolved from my own experiences, questions and navigations of faith. I grew up in the Deep South where my family regularly attended a Christian Baptist church; altar calls, revival meetings and attempts to sit still in a pew were a consistent part of my childhood. I left my hometown to attend college in California, and after graduation attended a non-denominational church that expanded my views on Christianity and spirituality. Over time, my theological beliefs have evolved, but the concept of purpose ("God's will" or "calling") has been continually on my mind, generating questions in both my personal and professional life. After a corporate job ended, I decided to become a substitute teacher, which led to my career change into the field of education. I eventually moved back to the South to complete my master's degree in education and entered the world of academia at a large, public institution.

Years later, I returned to the same public university to begin a doctoral program, and as a graduate teaching assistant had education students of my own. In the fall of 2011, one of my undergraduate students, Heidi (pseudonym), shared how her Christian beliefs had created challenges for her within her education program. I wondered how she was coping with her student teaching semester and e-mailed her to offer support. Below is a portion of her reply:

Hey Kim,

Well to be honest I am struggling! This is a lot harder than I thought it would be and I am always emotionally and even physically strained. I think I have so much going through my head all the time: Is this really for me? Is this my calling? Is this really what I want to do with my life? Will it be better when I have my own classroom or will I always struggle so much? . . . What's the point?

(Reprinted with permission)

I had encountered other Christian students who wrestled with issues of purpose during student teaching. Certainly a non-religious student could have written this e-mail. However, I understood from our conversations that she considered teaching a vocation and an extension of her faith. These questions were interwoven with her religious beliefs, and I wondered how she and other students mediated their religious identity within the context of their work.

Heidi's e-mail relayed her desire for clarity as she wrestled with significant life and identity questions. Specifically, what caught my attention was her mention of *calling*. Was teaching her calling? Since she associated calling with her Christian beliefs and mission, this was no small question. For her, student teaching was a critical time that would provide answers. How could I best support her, and what did *calling* really mean to her? These questions around calling and religious identity led me to develop a research study examining the meaning of calling for religious education students at a public institution. This study helped me better understand how a sense of calling can influence pre-service teachers' ideas about their purpose and role as teachers. Additionally, the interviews furthered my belief that discussion around the relationship between teaching and religion is needed within teacher education.

The Study

In the fall of 2012, I conducted a qualitative narrative study to explore how pre-service teachers' religious beliefs and views on calling influenced their experiences during their education programs, especially during the student teaching semester. The study examined the role of religious belief in the lives of four undergraduate pre-service teachers. Central research questions were: 1) How do religious student teachers define and think about teaching as a calling? 2) How do their meanings and perspectives influence their experiences in the context of their work at a public university?

Methods

To investigate these questions, I interviewed participants six times over a five-month period. I also asked that they keep a reflective journal in order to capture their thoughts after interviews and during their student teaching experience. Interview questions addressed the three-dimensional narrative inquiry space as described by Clandinin and Connelly (2000), examining the participants' experiences as they looked "inward and outward," "backward and forward," and located them "in place" (p. 54). Narrative inquiry provided a way to understand the intersection of participants' religious understandings and their evolving identities as teachers. Interviews took place during their student teaching semester beginning with questions surrounding their personal histories. We discussed their views on calling and the intersection of their Christian beliefs and teaching in subsequent interviews.

Participants

All of the participants were early childhood education majors (PreK–5th grade) at a large, public university in the southeastern United States, self-identified as Christians and viewed teaching as a calling or felt called to teach. On a preliminary recruitment questionnaire, 30 of the 35 early childhood students surveyed identified as a Christian in some way or with a Christian denomination. On the same questionnaire, education students were asked what they would tell someone to help that person "know" them. The participants I recruited all listed their Christian faith as an important part of that knowing, which led me to believe they would be open about the intersection of their faith and teaching. As Table 5.1 reveals, the participants were all in their early twenties, female and traditional undergraduate students completing their senior year of college.

The predominance of white (McDonald, 2007), middle-class (Hill-Jackson, 2007; McLean, 1999) women (E.W. Chizhik & A.W. Chizhik, 2005) in the teaching workforce is well documented. However, research suggests that another identity category, "Christian," could also be added to this list (Kimball, Mitchell, Thornton, & Young-Demarco, 2009). Yet, there is a scarcity of research providing religious women a space to share their views on the intersection of their faith and teaching.

TABLE 5.1 Background Information on Participants

Pseudonym/Religious identification	Age	Student teaching assignment	Ethnicity
Amy	22	Fifth grade	Caucasian
Follower of Jesus/Christian		Small, rural community	
Mary	22	First grade	Caucasian
Christian		Small, rural community	
Sarah	21	First grade	Caucasian
Christian/Methodist		Small, rural community	
Olivia	22	Fifth grade	Caucasian
Christian/Baptist		Small, rural community	

I offer my study to further the dialogue around the import of teachers' religious beliefs in the field of education, inviting Christian women themselves into the conversation.

The initial interviews quickly revealed the influence of Christianity in their lives, and it is from this context—the details of these first meetings—that I begin the conversation of the import of religious understandings in the lives of these pre-service teachers.

Amy

I first met Amy on a Sunday morning at a local coffee shop. She was outgoing and friendly, and I felt an immediate kinship with her. Amy described her Christian religious beliefs in terms of her personal relationship with Jesus Christ. She was not comfortable with the term "religion" because her faith was about her *relationship* with God, not about what she called "the more legalistic things of the church." She spoke of a transformative Christian faith, a faith that affected her daily life by her "striving to be more Christ-like" and "live in a manner the same way that He [Christ] did." Amy attended church regularly, served in the children's ministry, had assumed leadership roles in a university campus ministry and attended several Christian small groups.

Amy decided to pursue a degree in early childhood education during her freshman year of college. She had initially pursued a degree in science education, but ultimately felt a content-specific education degree was not the right choice for her. She had also considered an undergraduate degree in gifted education, but the university did not offer such a degree, so she decided on early childhood as a major. She wanted to teach because she felt she was gifted in teaching and leading, loved people and children, and wanted to build relationships in order to show others love.

Mary

Mary arrived for our first meeting at the same coffee shop accompanied by a guide dog she was training, and we began the first interview as the dog rested at her feet. It was easy to talk with Mary, as she was outgoing and forthright. Mary also described her Christian religious beliefs in terms of her relationship with Jesus Christ. She had attended the same church since she was seven, a non-denominational Christian church with a Wesleyan influence. Ministry had a strong influence in her family: her maternal grandparents were pastors, her youngest brother planned to become a pastor, her father led a men's group, and Mary said she was "really involved" with her church. She worshipped and prayed regularly and had participated in a foreign mission organization that included "discipleship training." Mary said, "I look to God for plans. I look to God for help ... I guess my relationship with him, with Jesus, is just like a part of me in my everyday life."

Mary had begun her undergraduate education degree at a different state college, but had been unhappy with the program. Frustrated with life, and searching for meaning and direction, Mary decided to take six months off from college and attend a ministry training school in Australia. She described asking God for direction and felt like she received it once in Australia, because "everything" she was assigned to do at the ministry school involved children or schools. During this time abroad, she decided that if her transfer application to her current early childhood program was accepted, she would view it as direction from God and would continue on to become a teacher.

Sarah

Sarah and I first met at the entrance of the College of Education building late on a Thursday afternoon. Sarah struck me as a soft-spoken and reserved young woman, but her initial shyness eventually disappeared as I got to know her. Sarah was thoughtful in her responses and came across as trustworthy because of the way she listened carefully and considered each question, and her overall demeanor gave the impression that she was kind.

Sarah had attended church "her whole life" and called her Christian faith "the core" of her family. She described her religious beliefs as:

> what gets me up in the morning and what makes it worthwhile for me to get through the day, because without it, I don't feel like there would be any real reason or joy to life. I'd just feel empty if I didn't have my faith.

Sarah's religious practice included prayer, reading the Bible and being a leader in a campus ministry organization. She used the example of the Christian cross to explain her faith and its influence on her life. The vertical axis represented her connection with God and "doing stuff for Him"; the horizontal axis represented her relationships with others and "just being a good example for them, not shoving stuff down their throat"; and the center symbolized her personal relationship with God.

Sarah knew prior to college that she would major in early childhood education and began planning her education coursework freshman year. She wanted to teach because of her love of children, and chose early childhood because she believed early childhood teachers are the ones who put students on "the right track."

Olivia

I first met Olivia at the elementary school where she was completing her student teaching, the setting for all but one of our meetings. When Olivia came to the school's front office, I observed how she already seemed to be a natural part of the school community. There was something immediately reassuring about her; she seemed sweet and kind, and had a no-nonsense way about her that seemed fitting for an elementary classroom.

Olivia also described her Christian faith as a part of her everyday life, calling it what she "clings on to." She stated:

> I think to me, my beliefs really do get me through a lot of hard times, a lot of challenges, a lot of even good times. Because it'll be something you praise, if something great or a blessing happens in your life, then I'll go and I'll praise God for that because I know it may not have been something I really did to deserve—or didn't have all these steps leading up to it, it just seems like it happened. And so those are extra blessings that I'm thankful for and to me, that is something God is doing, it's not just out of nowhere. I don't believe in coincidence.

Olivia was a leader in a campus ministry organization and frequently went on mission trips; she went every spring break while in college and stated, "I just love the opportunity to get to help people."

Olivia originally began her degree in English education, but switched to early childhood after a positive experience in one of her education classes that involved teaching young children. She said she wanted to help students learn, reach their goals and develop their "passions." Olivia also described wanting students to view her as someone who cares for them and wants them to be successful.

Data Analysis

I use the concept of *narratives of teaching* as an analytic lens to think about and explore the prevailing narratives at work in the participants' storytelling. This analytic tool was useful in looking across each story to ask questions such as: What stories does each woman tell about how her religious understandings and understandings about teaching overlap? How might each woman's religious understandings and sense of calling shape her ideas about her purpose and role as a teacher? Did the women have opportunities to discuss the relationship between their teaching and religious beliefs?

I was not looking for any narrative in particular; however, certain patterns and themes emerged. I initially sorted the participants' responses into categories such as: calling; faith and teaching; faith and teacher education. This analysis helped me begin the process of finding patterns in the women's stories. I then went through each subsidiary research question and highlighted text according to each question, and there were many occasions when sections of the texts addressed more than one research question. I then looked across the participants' stories for each question, which resulted in the creation of themes.

Data analysis suggests these aspiring teachers' Christian religious beliefs shape their thinking about teaching both in the reasons they give for choosing the teaching profession and in the visions they hold about the role of the teacher. Their *narratives of calling* included beliefs about *innate ability*, as well as beliefs about teaching as *love and care*. I also discovered despite the religious homogeneity of their cohort and some talk in courses about the influence of their Christian faith, there was limited opportunity to discuss the intersection of teaching and their religious understandings.

I soon discovered that *calling* is a word that elicits powerful connotations and is appropriated in different ways, which of course makes it difficult to know exactly what teachers mean when they say, "Teaching is my calling." However, as I looked across the stories of the participants, commonalities emerged. First, their definitions of calling were not simplistic, but nuanced and fluid. They described *teaching as a calling* in terms of their innate abilities or gifting. All participants (with the exception of Sarah) did not permanently link calling with teaching—calling was influenced by God's guidance and could change. The participants also framed calling in a way that aligned with their desire to teach. Second, their stories surrounding *teaching as a calling* often focused on the relational aspect of teaching. Loving and caring for students, and sometimes other teachers, was central to their role and purpose as teachers.

Innate Ability, a Sense of Guidance and Desire

When it came to viewing *teaching as a calling*, all the participants linked calling with innate skills or "gifts" which led them to their work with children and education. Amy believed God gives individuals "gifts" and "using those strengths that you have is kind of like following your calling." Mary said God gives us "certain gifts" to use for the purpose "He has for our life," but clarified that there was not just "one purpose" for her life. Sarah believed she was created with a natural ability to teach and said, "with the whole calling thing, I really think that it's just this innate gift in me to be able to interact with children." Olivia used the word "passion" to describe "calling," and linked it to what she was "good at." She said, "I think that's where . . . the passion and the gifting go hand in hand . . . realizing I'm good at this, which is hard to do sometimes because you don't want to brag on yourself."

It was only Sarah who stated unequivocally that she was "called to teach elementary students in public schools." For the others, a specific calling, such as teaching, was likely to change over time. "Calling" could include a sense of guidance from God toward an occupation, a reference to a more general gifting or ability, or a general sense of purpose like loving or serving others. There were nuances to their definitions, and "calling" was not always fixed.

Calling was also linked to desire and choice. Amy said, "I feel like I'm good with people, and I love to have relationships . . . so I think that kind of turned my focus towards the teaching realm." She talked about not wanting to limit herself to "one calling" saying, "I have lots of other desires of things that I would like to do too."

Mary also talked about her views regarding God and choice. Even though she defined calling as "what you feel like God has told you to do, the purpose that He has given you in your life," Mary did not believe God *mandated* these purposes or tasks. She explained:

> [M]y Dad describes it in this awesome little analogy where he says, God gives you a fence, boundary inside a playground . . . you can play on the slide or you can play on the swings or you can play on whatever part of the playground you want as long as you stay within the boundaries.

Mary talked about how her gifting and desires were related. She said, "I think [my purpose in life] . . . has to do with my giftings and . . . the desires that He's given me. I desire to teach, and I don't think He would have given me that desire if it wasn't something He wanted me to do." Sarah was very driven by her desire or "passion" to teach. She described her calling as a teacher, stating:

> I've always referred to it as just my passion, and that's what I'm very, very passionate about. That's what my heart yearns for, if you want to be poetic or something. But that's always how I've called it. I have the majority of my life called it a calling, or a gift from God, is what I would refer to it as.

Again, there was the expression of a desire to teach that was interwoven with calling. Olivia also referred to teaching as a "passion," and as stated earlier, talked about how passion and gifting go hand in hand.

Teaching as Love and Care

The relational aspect of teaching was interwoven in the participants' stories about calling and purpose. There was a common focus on loving students, which was often conflated with their views regarding their purposes and roles as Christian women.

Amy said she would be able to demonstrate God's love through her relationships with students and other teachers. She said:

> [T]eaching is such a relational profession and so through those relationships, even just living out what I believe is kind of a testament to that. And so even if I don't get to specifically have a conversation with these kids or have the ability to talk to them about it [her relationship with God], it's still something that I can show them, that love. The love that God has poured

out on me, I can give that to them and even if I don't have the opportunity to actually have in-depth conversations with them about it.

She thought her religious views would influence *the way* she taught, more than *what* she taught. Amy mentioned that teachers, like Christians, are meant to sacrifice, be selfless and serve others.

Mary felt God wanted her to support students and be "someone who they know they can come to with any issues." She stated that "obviously" she needed to help students learn "what they need to learn," but beyond that she wanted to love and care for them. She said most Christian women who seek "a relationship with Jesus" are kind-hearted and want to help people and are perhaps influenced by Jesus' example—He lived to help people, teach people, and also loved children.

Sarah said her Christian faith influences her to "continuously try to be mindful of how" she loves students. She said, "teaching is what I want to do, and being there for those kids is what my whole goal every single day is, and so technically, it's because of my religion that I'm doing that every day." Sarah said her calling was to make the students "feel loved, and important, and know they can succeed."

Olivia, like the others, expressed her desire to care for and love children. She also wanted to help students learn, develop their passions, and reach their goals. At one point Olivia talked about the service aspects of Christian ministry, and I asked her "if ministry is an act of service, what is teaching?" She replied, "It's also an act of service" and said:

> Both are kind of an act of service without really expecting anything in return. I mean yes, you get paid for teaching but besides that point, what you do outside of that where you are helping students, helping families, you're not expecting to get that in return as a teacher.

The participants understood their responsibility to help students learn academic skills and content, but beyond that, there was a sense of commitment to developing positive relationships with students that were intentional, and perhaps at times, sacrificial.

Conditions and Considerations

The participants' religious understandings and sense of calling influenced their views on their purpose and role as teachers. Their understanding of *calling* and narratives of *teaching as love and care* and *teaching as innate ability*, may be bolstered by three factors: the religious homogeneity of the women's cohort, the conflation of the women's narratives with prevailing narratives of primary education, and the lack of critical dialogue surrounding religious understandings.

Jesus and Rainbows: Religious Homogeneity

When I asked Mary about her early childhood education classes, she mentioned that approximately "75%" or "80%" of students in her cohort were Christian. Mary stated:

> [I]t's so weird that all of us—or most all of us are Christians . . . going into this major . . . I remember meeting this one girl . . . she's in a cohort before me . . . she was complaining about how everything is Jesus and rainbows . . . And she was just complaining that all they do in her cohort was talk about happy things all the time and Jesus.

Indeed, the women in the study did come from a cohort of pre-service teachers who identified in similar ways. Diversity did exist, but in terms of religion most identified as Christian. Amy talked about the "really cool group of girls" in her cohort who she knew "also loved the Lord" and who "encouraged each other a lot." Mary said, "as soon as I got into the program, I was like, oh my gosh. This is awesome. We all pretty much have the same basic beliefs . . . I just thought it was really interesting." Sarah said, "There's a lot of people in this major [early childhood] that are very active in their faith in different ministries across the campus."

In some ways, the homogeneity is not surprising as many college students proceed through their programs of study surrounded by peers who identify in similar ways (Bécares & Turner, 2004; Kimball et al., 2009). Kimball et al. (2009) found college students recognize, at least to some degree, the different worldviews associated with majors and may self-sort accordingly. For example, Bohlmeyer, Burke, and Helmstadter (as cited in Bécares & Turner, 2004, p. 468) claim education majors are more emotionally empathetic than business majors. Other research indicates that "highly religious people seem to prefer Education majors" (Kimball et al., 2009, p. 22).

On one hand, such a context may allow students to more readily share experiences with peers; they may feel a sense of common purpose and commitment to the field. Mary described her teacher education classes as a place where fellow students were open about their religious faith and "no one was afraid to be like hey, I'm a Christian, or hey, I'm Jewish or whatever." Amy mentioned the benefit of reading the Bible and praying with another Christian student teacher during their commute to their field placement. Sarah said, "having more in common" made it more comfortable for her to relate to students in her cohort.

On the other hand, a lack of religious diversity may silence peers who do not share the same views, and create limited opportunity to hear divergent religious views in education classes. Even though I did not interview non-Christians in this cohort, we can infer from the "Jesus and rainbows" comment that some students may find such religious homogeneity problematic. If like-minded peers surround college students, one concern is that they adequately consider divergent viewpoints, especially in the case of pre-service teachers who go on to teach diverse student populations.

Conflating Narratives

Christian women may self-sort into primary education because Christian narratives of service, love and sacrifice overlap with many of the cultural teaching myths as described by Britzman. Britzman (2003) states, "Like the 'good' woman, the 'good' teacher is positioned as self-sacrificing, kind, overworked, underpaid, and holding an unlimited reservoir of patience" (p. 28).

These narratives of care and sacrifice endure within primary education for a reason. Many scholars (Apple, 1988; Bennett & LeCompte, 1990; Grumet, 1988; Preston, 1993) have pointed to connections between teaching, childcare and conceptions of femininity. Preston (1993) stated, "Over the course of the nineteenth century . . . teaching became women's work not only statistically but ideologically and prescriptively as well, an activity no longer properly within the realm of male endeavor" (p. 532). The ideology of domesticity influenced the argument that "the most effective teacher would draw upon the female qualities of emotionality, maternal love, gentleness, and moral superiority" (p. 532).

Horace Mann, the father of the common school movement and Massachusetts' secretary of education, believed women possessed innate qualities that made them natural teachers of children (Mann, 1853). Mann weaved domesticity, childcare and morality throughout his views on women and emphasized the strong correlation between women's nature and teaching. He stated:

> [T]he most honorable and beneficent employment in civilized society is emphatically hers. I mean the education of children. That women should be the educator of children, I believe to be as much a requirement of nature as that she should be a mother of children. . . . The teacher's work is heart-work; yea, in the very core of the heart.
>
> (Mann, 1853, pp. 82–83)

The notion that women are natural teachers and that teaching is heart-work endures today, as evident in the participants' narratives of innate ability, love, service and care; again, narratives also found within Christian teachings. In many ways, the number of Christian women drawn to primary education should not be surprising since these narratives overlap.

Space to Talk

The influence of these narratives and the import of the participants' religious understandings are worthy of discussion. Yet, the women reported limited opportunity to critically think about or discuss the intersection of their religious understandings and teaching within the context of their education classes. Furthermore, they seemed to benefit from speaking about their Christian beliefs during the interviews. When asked about the interview process, Amy stated it helped her understand and reflect upon her beliefs. Mary also found the experience "revealing." Sarah said she was "able to more finely develop" her thoughts about how religion and school "intertwine," and Olivia found it caused her to reflect and think, "Oh, I didn't think about that."

Having this space to talk and reflect seemed to generate questions and at times, new understandings. Beyond reflection, most of the participants expressed uncertainty towards the more pragmatic (and legal) classroom concerns when it came to issues of religious belief. Mary wanted to better understand "the rules" in public schools like:

> What can we say, what can't we say, what are responses that we can say when some of our students bring up God or that they don't celebrate this, or that they don't do that or whatever. Just what we can and can't say or examples ... just more guidance in it.

She said if a student asked her about her faith, she would have "no clue" regarding how to respond. Sarah also mentioned not sufficiently understanding what is allowed in a public school setting:

> [I]t's such a taboo subject that they [faculty] won't even really address it and I feel like that they should at least address that idea instead of—the only way they'll bring it up is just to say, if you're not sure, don't do it ... And I think that that's very unrealistic because things like that come up almost every week, especially in the South with such a strong Christian population. Kids will constantly bring up Jesus and God and they can relate it to almost any subject ... I think the College of Ed should prepare ... a little more for that.

Olivia also mentioned not knowing what she could talk about in terms of her religious beliefs in a public school, and said, "We never sat down and looked at here's what the actual laws are."

The Personal and the Professional: A Christian and a Teacher

For these young women, their religious understandings were a part of their everyday lives and influenced how they viewed their roles and responsibilities as teachers. This study supports the argument that personal and professional identities cannot be separated. According to Baurain (2012):

> [S]piritual and religious beliefs demonstrably find their way into how teachers know what they know and why they do what they do (White, 2009,

2010). Elements of personal faith might affect classroom decision making, relationships with students, professional development priorities, and overall pedagogy . . . An expansion in this area of the nexus among personal and professional beliefs, identities, and practices is overdue.

(p. 313)

The conflation of the participants' personal and professional identities can be seen in how their *narratives about teaching* and *their narratives about being Christians* overlapped. Religion is certainly not the only influence in these women's lives—issues of identity are, of course, complex. However, what we can conclude from these women's stories is the need for more discussion around the import of teachers' (both pre-service and in-service) religious understandings. Even though education students may be talking about their Christian beliefs with one another or during class introductions, it is unclear as to the degree their beliefs are discussed within the formal content of education courses. There may not be sufficient opportunity to discuss the import and influence of their religious beliefs, for themselves and their students.

It is difficult to conclude what may hinder the discussion of religious beliefs within teacher education. Perhaps, as Sarah states, religion is simply a taboo subject. Or perhaps, educators do not know how to begin the conversation. At any rate, White (2009) argues that some education students want to discuss religion, but do not have the space to do so, and perhaps in-service teachers would like this opportunity as well. Certain narratives of teaching (teaching as a calling; teaching as innate ability; teaching as love and care) seemed to be furthered by the contexts in this study. There needs to be more discussion on what these narratives *do*, to the teachers who adopt them and to the students in their classrooms as well as what may hinder discussion of these topics and how we might encourage self-reflexivity, understanding and dialogue.

References

Apple, M.W. (1988). *Teachers and texts: A political economy of class and gender relations in education.* New York: Routledge.

Baurain, B. (2012). Beliefs into practice: A religious inquiry into teacher knowledge. *Journal of Language, Identity, and Education, 11*(5), 312–332.

Bécares, L., & Turner, C. (2004). Sex, college major, and attribution of responsibility in empathic responding to persons with HIV infection. *Psychological Reports, 95*(2), 467–476.

Bennett, K.P., & LeCompte, M.D. (1990). *The ways schools work: A sociological analysis of education.* New York: Longman.

Britzman, D.P. (2003). *Practice makes practice: A critical study of learning to teach* (rev. ed.). Albany, NY: State University of New York Press.

Chizhik, E.W., & Chizhik, A.W. (2005). Are you privileged or oppressed? Students' conceptions of themselves and others. *Urban Education, 40*(2), 116–143.

Clandinin, D.J., & Connelly, F.M. (2000). *Narrative inquiry: Experience and story in qualitative research.* San Francisco, CA: Jossey-Bass.

Grumet, M.R. (1988). *Bitter milk: Women and teaching.* Amherst, MA: The University of Massachusetts Press.

Hamachek, D. (1999). Effective teachers: What they do, how they do it, and the importance of self-knowledge. In R.P. Lipka & T.M. Brinthaupt (Eds.), *The role of self in teacher development* (pp. 189–224). Albany, NY: State University of New York Press.

Hill-Jackson, V. (2007). Wrestling whiteness: Three stages of shifting multicultural perspectives among White pre-service teachers. *Multicultural Perspectives, 9*(2), 29–35.

Kimball, M.S., Mitchell, C.M., Thornton, A.D., & Young-Demarco, L.C. (2009). Empirics on the origins of preferences: The case of college major and religiosity. *National Bureau of Economic Research,* Working Paper No. 15182. Retrieved from http://www.nber.org/papers/w15182

Mann, H. (1853). A *few thoughts on the powers and duties of woman: Two lectures.* Syracuse, NY: Hall, Mills, and Company.

McDonald, M.A. (2007). The joint enterprise of social justice teacher education. *Teachers College Record, 109*(8), 2047–2081.

McLean, S.V. (1999). Becoming a teacher: The person in process. In R.P. Lipka & T. M Brinthaupt (Eds.), *The role of self in teacher development* (pp. 55–91). Albany, NY: State University of New York Press.

Preston, J.A. (1993). Domestic ideology, school reformers, and female teachers: Schoolteaching becomes women's work in nineteenth-century New England. *The New England Quarterly, 66*(4), pp. 531–551.

White, K. (2009). Connecting religion and teacher identity: The unexplored relationship between teachers and religion in public schools. *Teaching and Teacher Education, 25*(6), 857–866.

6

FISHING BELOW THE SURFACE

Understanding the Role of Religion in Student Learning

Simone Schweber

Guiding Questions:

In what ways do students' religious understandings inform their learning experiences?
How might teachers recognize and engage students' religious understandings as inherent to their identities and experience as learners?

When the World Trade Towers fell in New York City, I happened to be doing research in a charismatic, evangelical, fundamentalist Christian school. I was visiting the school daily, sitting in the back of an eighth-grade class. In the days immediately after the attacks, the teacher talked with the students about the meaning of those events, struggling sometimes to interpret how they fit into God's plan, but absolutely sure that they did. When there were still survivors being pulled out of the rubble, this teacher taught her students that those survivors who had accepted Jesus as their savior were not in pain. They may be hurting physically, but they were not in psychic pain, she seemed to imply. They knew that their lives were in God's hands, and they knew that they were saved, that even were they to die, their lives were meaningful, part of a religious system that ordered the world. As a result, no matter where they were, no matter in what condition, they were not in pain; at least their bodies were not in the same pain as they would be if they were unsaved.

That classroom discussion was surprising to me at the time. I hadn't known a lot about fundamentalist Christians, and I was surprised by what I came to think of as that teacher's theological certainty. I was surprised that this teacher would claim to know what those survivors were feeling, bodily or psychically. I doubted this teacher's beliefs despite the fact that I had grown up with an extended family of very firm believers. Though they were orthodox Jews rather than fundamentalist Christians, they, like this teacher, had a very focused relationship to a single God. They knew or perhaps were always striving to know and to act according to God's wishes, dictates and guidelines; and moreover, they had a very clear sense of how those made their lives meaningful, their pain tolerable and their joys abundant.

It's perhaps as a result of this family connection that I came to be interested in religious education in the first place, specifically in religious students' ideas. On 9/11/2001, I was studying religious education in part because I wanted to understand how religious kids' religious notions shape their thinking about the world writ large.

Since doing that study, I've come to think that there are multiple ways in which religious ideas shape students' interactions with the school curriculum, but that they can be distilled into three big categories: conscious, self-conscious and unconscious. There are the ways that students' religious worldviews shape their curricular experience very consciously (for them), there are times when not only are those identities conscious but they make students feel very self-conscious, and there are times when they are simply "unconscious" of their interpretation being religiously driven. While I'm using these psychological terms a little glibly, I mean them quite seriously.

Consciously Religious

Students can be very conscious of aspects of their religious identities during school, and not only because they wear special dress or hope to pray at particular hours. The substance of their religious identities can come to the fore intellectually during coverage of what might be called "religious-identity" issues—ideas that surface particularities of their religious beliefs, practices or any aspect of their lives.

As an example, consider the case of Lila, a Jewish, third-grade girl, whose class was studying a series of units about large-scale violence. Lila was a participant in a research study I conducted on how students in the early grades learn about genocide and how it impacts them intellectually and psychologically. When the third graders studied the genocide of the Arawak Indians, Lila was moved, she was interested and she was involved, but she didn't feel that her own religious identity mattered particularly. When the students studied the dropping of bombs on Hiroshima and Nagasaki, again, she was interested and studied hard, but again, she didn't feel that she was personally involved somehow. The unit after these, however, focused on the Holocaust, and Lila, as a Jewish girl, identified with Anne Frank when they read and watched a film about her. Unlike the prior units, this unit for Lila felt personal. In talking about learning this unit as a third grader, Lila reported, "I get really sad, and I just . . . get all depressed and stuff, hearing about these people who, I mean, if I were born 50 years ago, this could have been me!" (Schweber, 2008, p. 2097). Lila's being Jewish here mattered; it was part of her conscious identity. Her youth, her Jewishness and the social studies curriculum all played a part in her becoming seriously depressed by the content she was learning. Lila stopped playing with her cats, she stopped rough-housing with her brother, and her parents sought out the school counselor to help her talk through her nightmares about the Holocaust.

When the subject matter consciously invokes aspects of students' religious identities, of course the results are not always distressing. Sometimes, students can be especially interested in what they are learning in school because it accords with something they learned at their Kingdom Hall (if they're Jehovah's Witnesses) or because it conflicts with something they learned at their Buddhist temple. Interest and disinterest might be sparked by the curriculum due to students' sense of their religious commitments or loyalties. When these moments are *conscious* for students, they are easiest for us as teachers to address because they're on the table, so to speak.

When the kindergartener learning about primates casually mentions that because he is a Christian he doesn't believe that people came from monkeys, it's easy to elicit more information from him and to know that his religious identity is in play. As his kindergarten teacher I can ask him whether his whole family is Christian, whether he goes to church, what that's like, what he likes or doesn't like about it, what he thinks about monkeys and what he thinks people mean when they say that people "evolved" from them. Because he has paved the way for me to know that this is a religious belief for him, it's signaled speech for me; I know to tread lightly, to treat his religious ideas thoughtfully, but not to be afraid of discussing them, of sharing them, not to leave them "untouched" or disregarded out of nervousness or fear. Because part of my philosophy of education is that students' growth is better served when their whole identities can be surfaced in caring classrooms, I don't want to bury this student's religious ideas. I want to discuss them and in that way help this student consider them "intelligently" (Noddings, 1993). I don't want religion to be a taboo subject in schools, and likewise, I don't want students' religious identities to be.

Self-consciously Religious, Religiously Intersected

That said, when students' religious identities are "triggered" by the school curriculum, it's always worth remembering, as a teacher, that students can feel exceedingly self-conscious, and not only if their affiliation is a minority religion. Students can feel self-conscious about their religious beliefs or activities, their religious dress or friendships because of how their religious identity plays out *for them*, not only as it plays out in some abstract way in the classroom.

The Jewish student, Lila, to whom I referred above, encountered Holocaust lessons in her public high school classroom twelve years after her third-grade experience, and that early learning experience shaped her later on in powerful ways. Lila felt terribly self-conscious in tenth grade as one of the only Jewish students in the classroom, again. She wondered if the other, non-Jewish students in her class were sneaking glances at her as they learned about Jewish victimization. In that moment, she felt *self-consciously Jewish*. But it was not only because she was

Jewish that she felt self-conscious. It was also because she had had the experience of being the only Jewish student learning about the Holocaust when she was in third grade. Her tenth-grade experience evoked her third-grade experience; put differently, I imagine that had she not been the only Jewish girl in her public elementary school, she would likely have experienced the tenth-grade history class sessions differently.

As a more specific example, consider the middle school student whose two mothers divorced three years ago. The one mother is devoutly Catholic and white; though she disagrees with the Church's official stance on gay marriage, she is nonetheless dedicated to raising her child as a Catholic, attends mass weekly and wants her child to be confirmed in a few short years. The second mother is a member of the African Methodist Episcopal (AME) Zion church and is black; she dislikes Catholicism intensely for its racist history, for the way her marriage was not recognized by the Church and for its hierarchical authoritarian structure. This mother looks forward to becoming an elder and hopes that her child will remain an active member of her church.

Imagine that in school, while studying the birth of the Civil Rights movement, this student learns about Ralph David Abernathy and the Southern Christian Leadership Conference. For that child learning about Ralph David Abernathy and his leading the March on Washington in the wake of Martin Luther King's assassination, the history is a trigger for questions of religious identity, but obviously not only of religious identity. Put differently, the questions of religious identity are not solely religious. It's easy to imagine that, for this child, the questions of religious identity are bound up in ethnicity, loyalty, the dynamics of divorce and the specifics of geography. This child being raised in San Francisco would be living in a different country, in essence, than this "same" imagined child growing up in Southern Indiana. Or, when this child has had a fight with one mother, the child may feel more likely to embrace Catholicism, and when the child has fought with the other mother, more likely to embrace AME. Either way, the child's curricular learning has the opportunity to be a powerful trigger of self-consciousness in the classroom, of confusion, resistance and sadness and in equal measure, empowerment, clarity, authentic learning and pride.

In short, our students are probably never working out their ideas about religion in isolation from their ideas about their worlds in general. They are working out their religious ideas and commitments in concert with their social groups, their familial groups, their social class and economic aspirations, their personal histories and societal conflicts, their homes, neighborhoods and homelands, their hormones, disabilities, superpowers and worldviews, their religious leaders, relationships to their teachers and classroom dynamics.

What are we to do with this kind of complexity as teachers? I have an answer, however imperfect. When students feel self-consciously religious—that is, when their religious identities are felt to be on display somehow, at issue, invoked or provoked, in all their complexities, in our classrooms, we ought to aim to do what we aim to do generally. We have to aim to surface the issues at play, caringly, clearly but unabashedly.

Imagine that our imagined biracial child from this scenario is angry, that learning about the courage of Abernathy feels like a betrayal of one mother and an endorsement of the other. Let's imagine that in class, the student throws the book, literally, at me as the teacher. (I always like to imagine a best-case scenario in the wake of violent acts; it's a habit formed from studying genocide that I think helps to figure out what move to make next.) I imagine sending this child out of the classroom, tending to my bruised face and sense of public humiliation, and I especially like to imagine that there is enough support in the school to allow me as the teacher to talk to this student later, quietly, alone in a room, before any consequences are involved.

"Can you talk me through what happened?" I like to imagine asking this young person (whose name I would of course know). "Can you let me know what you were thinking or feeling in class?" And though this is an idealized imagining, I like to think that this child, with guidance, time and genuine care, would be able to apologize, maybe not immediately, but eventually, after figuring out and considering the many-layered emotions that exploded in that moment. I like to think that my student would open up, would continue the struggle to figure out rational responses to living in an unfair world and would start the hard work of regulating impulses.

Do I think this would be an easy discussion to have? No. Would it require me as the teacher to be patient and compassionate and more than a little selfless and calm? Yes. Does this mean that we as teachers should get trained as therapists and guidance counselors and substitute love-providers and non-violence experts with schools filled with kids who have been traumatized by circumstance, all of whom deserve alone-time with us? Probably. But I am asking us to do this as teachers because I think we can, not always, not even necessarily most of the time, but sometimes, and it's those of us who want to do this kind of work when we can who should be teaching in the places that need us. I find it helpful to remember this; when students are self-conscious in our classrooms about their intersectional identities, it is not our job to heal them. We need to do our best, however, to accept them in all their complexities and to guide them towards wholeness whenever possible. I can imagine being Lila's high school history teacher, for example, and hoping that I would have asked her how it felt to learn about the Holocaust as one of the few Jews in the classroom, and that even that small act—the act of asking—would allow her to feel less alone religiously, socially, humanly. I would not need to share her religious identity to make her feel less alone in the room.

Unconsciously Religious

These imagined scenarios are of course utterly idealized, especially given the limited time teachers have for genuine caring of students. But they're also idealized in that they assume that students can actually articulate the ways in which their religious identities are present in the classroom. My suspicion is that it is hardest, as teachers, to deal with the exceedingly complex ways that students' religious identities shape their understandings of curricular material, not consciously or self-consciously, but *unconsciously*, when students don't think of their ideas as being connected to their religious commitments.

Imagine the Mormon in your class. While she has many, many ideas that are rooted in her religion and that she's thereby conscious of as such, she also has vague notions that come from her religious worldview but that she doesn't necessarily think of as stemming from the culture of Mormonism or from the values that the Church of Jesus Christ of Latter Day Saints inculcates. As a Mormon, she may think of poverty not as an individual affliction but as a collective responsibility. (Mormons generally try to follow Roger Smith's model of caring for the mostly poor farmers who were his first followers.) So this student may think that money is not an end in itself and not particularly valuable as a marker of success. Money might be good to have, but it is always important to tithe and to remember that no one Mormon is better than another. Contrast this general orientation towards wealth and poverty with someone who prays at a mega-church in which the leader preaches Prosperity theology (a variant of Christian Protestantism). The teenager who grows up as a dedicated follower of Prosperity theology might believe that wealth is a blessing that God bestows on the deserving and that people in poverty need to actively avoid thinking of themselves as "victims." These two students' views of poverty and wealth, the values and causes of both, might be radically different even though both may be subconscious or unconscious. Imagine these two students sitting quietly in an American history classroom, learning about the stock market crash of 1929. While they may seem to be studying the same content, listening to the same teacher, and reading the same materials, they may still have radically different value judgments about the meaning of the events they are studying.

I recently taught an immigrant student who had come from Malaysia. He was a practicing Buddhist, and he thought that the entire history curriculum of American schools had a strangely individualistic bias; as a Buddhist, he considered feelings and actions and beliefs not to be generally the domain of the individual, and certainly never explicable at the individual level, but instead to be generally more collectivist. Students may consider history itself as generally moving towards "progress" or "decline"—which may also be an artifact of their religious traditions. Even the appropriateness or rightness of having a religious leader—like a Pope—may mean that devout Catholic students consider leadership, generally, to be commonplace rather than a human mistake. There are all kinds of values that students subconsciously or unconsciously inherit from their religious traditions that may or may not make it to the level of educational discourse, but instead stay submerged, looming large in students' meaning-making but staying silent in classroom conversation.

What Do We Do as Teachers? Go Fish

In this chapter, I argue that students' religious identities matter in their interpretations of what they're learning, and that sometimes, necessarily, as teachers we miss the ways that those identities shape meaning-making in our classrooms. We just don't "see" that a student thinks of her disabled peer as inhabited by spirits, or specially blessed or punished by God for having gay parents. We don't realize that when learning about the Jewish Holocaust, a Palestinian student considers all Jews to be Israeli occupiers and the Holocaust to be a Jewish fiction. We don't see that the atheist feels left out or afraid to express his opinions in the conservative Christian district in which he lives. Sometimes these students' religiously infused ideas surface in our classrooms, but sometimes they don't. Our students hide them because they know that their ideas are sometimes politically incorrect, or because they are afraid that their ideas are unlike their peers', or they have already learned that school is not the place for such discussions. Our students may simply be unaware of their religiously laden interpretations, or maybe they just believe what they believe or do what they do as the people they are.

What do we do about that? I suggest that we do our utmost as teachers to raise these ideas and discuss them. I want us, as teachers, whether in public or private schools, to consider it part of our work to put religious ideas on the table. I want them to be part of classroom conversations, both as a way to deepen our students' learning and as a way to deepen our learning about our students and students' learning about each other.

I think of religiously infused ideas, whether conscious or not, as being somehow fishy—and here I don't mean that they are suspect, but that they are like fish, swimming below the surface of our typical classroom discussions. They may be beautiful or dangerous fish, large or small, fast or slow, camouflaged or bright, deep down in the depths or reflecting rays of the sun—but they do not always make it to the surface, where we teach. They don't always come up for air or light or examination. Whether students' religious identities are obvious or not—we still owe it to them to fish for their ideas, to bring them to the surface. We owe it to our students to try to raise those ideas up from the depths, not to swallow them whole, but simply to see them.

I think of this work as a form of teaching for social justice and democratic participation. When left unexamined, our deepest religious ideas sometimes stand in the way of our understanding each other; when discussed, the watery surface provides a slightly more level field, because no matter how briefly, all of our students' religious ideas float atop the ocean of possibilities. Examining these ideas in our classrooms helps us achieve social justice because it helps us see each other more clearly, and because it helps us see ourselves, sometimes with surprising clarity, too. Learning about ourselves and each other, our differences and commonalities, our religious commitments and confusions, has the capacity to make our democracy more robust as well. Because religion is a specially protected category in the U.S.

constitution, it is part of our constitution as a nation to argue through difficult religious dilemmas and for them to recur, not to be solved. We need to learn how to navigate these deep religious differences, and I believe that there is no place better to do that than in schools.

I sometimes think back to that school I was in on 9/11 (2001) and what the conversation might have looked like had the students I was observing in that eighth-grade class been able to discuss with kids from other religious worldviews what was happening. I like to imagine in particular that there could be Buddhist and Muslim and Hindu and Jewish and Mormon and Protestant and Catholic and agnostic and secular humanist and atheist kids from all over the world in that classroom, sitting together, talking and trying to make sense of what causes violence, how it might be overcome, how their religious identities help them make meaning and how it shapes their understandings of each other and the world. I don't imagine such discussions would be easy, but I do imagine that like deliberations of controversial issues and investigations of difficult subjects, done well and facilitated carefully and caringly, they have the power to change us in the most fundamental ways.

References

Noddings, N. (1993). *Educating for intelligent belief or unbelief.* The John Dewey Lecture. New York: Teachers College Press.

Schweber, S. (2008). 'What happened to their pets?': Third graders encounter the Holocaust. *Teachers College Record, 110*(10), 2073–2115.

7

RECONSIDERING RELIGION IN THE CURRICULUM

Keith C. Barton

Guiding Questions:

How does understanding religion prepare students for democratic life?
How do our religious backgrounds get in the way of understanding other religions?
What do schools usually leave out when they teach about religion?

Many educators have argued that in order to promote the tolerance, mutual respect and reasoned judgment necessary for participation in a pluralist democracy, schools should devote greater attention to developing students' understanding of religion (e.g. Green & Oldendorf, 2011; Nash & Bishop, 2010; Nord, 1995; Nord & Haynes, 1998). Familiarity with the world's religions is critical for a well-rounded understanding of history and contemporary society, as well as for participation in the public life of a democracy. Without knowing how religions shape values and attitudes, students will have little ability to comprehend or communicate with those from differing backgrounds. And without knowing more about religious ideas, themes and philosophies, students will fail to appreciate much of the world's art, literature and architecture, or understand some of its most important ethical systems. Yet this area of life, which is so important to so many people, is curiously absent in most textbooks and formal curricula in the United States, as well as in many other countries. Devoting greater attention to religion appears to be an obvious path to educating students who can make informed judgments and collaborate respectfully with others.

Unless educators think deeply about how they approach the topic, however, increasing the amount of attention given to religion may not lead to a better understanding of people and society. After all, schools already teach about religion to some extent, but they approach it in a way that may do more to limit students' perspectives than to expand them. Without examining the simplifications, distortions and omissions that occur in teaching about religion, increased coverage will fail to achieve the noble goals that are so often laid out for this area of study. This reconsideration requires addressing three significant shortcomings in current treatments: static and essentialized portrayals of world religions; ethnocentric interpretations of religions; and lack of attention to the political, social and psychological dimensions of religion. None of these shortcomings will be easy to overcome, and none can be tackled by teachers alone. Although suggestions for teaching are included in this chapter, a fuller reconsideration of religion in the curriculum also requires attention to curriculum guidelines, instructional materials, professional development and teacher education. Only with serious and sustained attention to the role of religion in each of these components of schooling can students develop a more meaningful and comprehensive understanding of the religious dimension of social life.

A Curricular Journey

When authors write about the role of religion in education, they often begin by talking about their personal journeys, just as Jennifer has done in the introduction to this volume. Educators often come to appreciate the importance of the topic because their own spiritual views have changed over time; perhaps they have struggled with the role of faith or organized religion in their lives, or they have overcome religious prejudices and blind spots. My own journey is a different one. Spirituality has never played a role in my life, and I feel no more tolerant or intolerant toward one religion than another. But as someone who prepares elementary and secondary teachers, I've found myself on a long journey to understand how we can best teach about this topic. I've struggled to make sense of both my own ideas and those of others: what it means to understand religion, why this can be so difficult and how our ideas change. This quest is based, in part, on the very different religious contexts in which I've found myself.

I grew up in a small Southern town. My family was Southern Baptist, and I went to Sunday School every week—earning 10 years' worth of perfect attendance pins along the way. Sometimes we turned out for Sunday night services or Wednesday prayer meetings, and my summers always included Vacation Bible School and revivals. Many of my friends went to other Protestant churches, and the town also had a small Catholic church, as well as a handful of Jewish families. Churches were central to the community, but religious belief wasn't a very pervasive part of most of my friends' lives. As teenagers, we didn't spend much time worrying about theology, even if we went to church regularly. Yet we certainly knew that many people were devout in their faith, and that their beliefs influenced how they lived—wearing certain clothes or hairstyles, disdaining celebrations or luxury goods, collecting food for the needy.

I grew up knowing that people's religious beliefs differed, and in college I encountered an even wider diversity of backgrounds. But the first time I remember being *surprised* by anyone's perspective on religion was in a graduate anthropology seminar in Los Angeles. The class had watched *The Holy Ghost People* (Boyd & Adair, 1968), a documentary on Appalachian snake-handlers. Most of my classmates had never met a fundamentalist Christian (and this was before the religious right featured so prominently in the media), so they refused to accept that the churchgoers were really putting themselves at risk by handling poisonous snakes; they thought it was just a hoax. I didn't doubt the snakes were poisonous, because I knew how important religion can be in people's lives and what lengths they go to in service to their faith. The rest of the class, though, couldn't imagine anyone risking their lives that way, and they regarded my defense of snake-handlers as small-town naïveté. I didn't understand how such well-educated people—on their way to becoming anthropologists—didn't see something that was so obvious to me.

Many years later, as an educational researcher, I spent quite a bit of time in Northern Ireland. This also led me to think about how people make sense of religion, and particularly its role in social and political life. Political conflicts in Northern Ireland routinely play out as opposition between two religious communities—Catholic and Protestant. Although theological differences between the two groups are minimal, their differing historical experiences and political allegiances overshadow similarities of faith. And disturbingly, the actions of people there—when they descend into prejudice, hatred and violence—contradict the very tenets of their Christianity. Northern Ireland isn't alone in this regard; religious violence has been a recurring theme in history, and it still plagues many areas of the world. I've struggled to understand how people can justify violent acts in the name of religions that extol the value of peace, and how we can educate our students so that they don't fall prey to such manipulation.

My most recent struggle with understanding religion has come during travel to South East Asia. I often visit temples when I'm there, and I also see a variety of religious symbols and practices in homes and businesses. It sometimes frustrates me that I can't make sense of what I see. I've always felt that I understood Judaism and Islam pretty well, because they're so similar to Christianity, and the three religions share the same historic roots. But I'm less successful at understanding practices associated with Hinduism, Buddhism, Taoism and Chinese folk religion. These are so different from my own background that I come up short when I try to compare them to Christianity. Sometimes they just don't fit my conceptual categories, and so my friends there have to put up with my constant questions. Two teachers in Singapore asked me why I was so interested in the subject. They clearly suspected I might be another confused Westerner looking for spiritual answers in exotic Eastern religions. My answer, they told me, was more satisfying. "I'm interested as a teacher," I said. "Religion has so much influence on the lives of people around the world that I want to know how we can do a better job of teaching about it." This chapter presents some of the conclusions I've reached during this curricular journey.

Teaching about Diversity and Change in World Religions

Students in the United States often study religion as part of world history and geography in the middle grades or later. The curriculum at this level typically requires coverage of "major world religions," which most often includes Christianity, Islam, Judaism, Buddhism, Confucianism and Hinduism, and occasionally other traditions such as Sikhism and Shinto. Teachers are expected to cover a number of important topics, such as the beliefs, scriptures and practices of each of these religions; their historical origins and diffusion; and sometimes their influence on art, architecture or other aspects of culture. In my experience working with pre-service and in-service teachers, I've been impressed with their sincerity in teaching about religions other than their own, but I've also been disappointed by their adherence to narrow curriculum guidelines and limited instructional materials. Ironically, some of the most problematic aspects of developing students' understanding of religion occur when schools most directly address the topic.

Moving Beyond the "Major" Religions

"Major" religions certainly deserve a great deal of attention, because they claim millions of adherents and have influenced social and political structures for centuries or millennia. However, religions that rarely make the list also have long histories and comparable numbers of adherents. These include Chinese folk religion, which is a dominant tradition in China and among Chinese migrants throughout the world (Chinese Folk Religion Adherents by Country, 2011; Goossaert, 2005), but which is almost never studied in U.S. schools. Similarly, Yoruba religion is widespread in West Africa and influences belief and practice among descendants of the African diaspora worldwide (Prothero, 2010), but it is unheard of in most curricula. Many millions of people also belong to less well-known religions (including local indigenous traditions), and about 16% of the world's population do not claim adherence to any organized religion—with about half of those identifying as completely nonreligious (Secular/Nonreligious/Agnostic/Atheist, 2013). Excluding these groups suggests that the only ways of organizing religious belief and practice are those found in a truncated list of "major" religions, and it also gives the mistaken impression that religious belief is universal.

In addition, focusing on a short list of religions limits students' understanding of social and cultural diversity in many world regions, and this leaves students vulnerable to the misleading stereotypes often found in the media. When a Kurdish girl in Iraq was stoned in 2007, for example, some reports portrayed this kind of "honor killing" as a feature of Muslim life (e.g. Susskind, 2007; cf. Terman, 2010). This particular Kurdish community, however, was not Muslim but Yazidi. Similarly, the media often implies that the Palestinian conflict pits Muslims against Jews, even though significant numbers of Palestinians are Christian, Druze or Samaritan (and many people from all sides condemn violence). Thinking of the

Middle East and neighboring countries as consisting only of Muslims (and, in Israel, of Jews) omits these other groups—Yazidis, Christians, Druze, Samaritans, but also Zorastrians, Bahaists, Mandeans and Shabaks. Nor do India and surrounding countries consist only of Hindus and Muslims; there are also Sikhs, Jains, Parsis, Christians, Buddhists and followers of local religious traditions. Students' exposure to religion in the curriculum should complicate their understanding of the diversity of these parts of the world, but focusing on a simplified list of major religions is more likely to reinforce overgeneralizations.

Of course, it isn't possible to teach about each of the world's thousands of religions, and as a teacher I would rebel at the thought that I had to know about them all. Schools can, however, take at least two important steps toward helping students better understand this diversity. First, the curriculum should acknowledge that there are many religions beyond the "major" ones, and that many people are not affiliated with any religion at all. In addition to studying the major religions in the middle grades, for example, students should have the opportunity to do group or individual projects on religions that lie outside these categories. No student will ever learn about all of them, but simply becoming aware of the existence of a greater range of religious diversity will help develop more complete and complex understandings of the topic. The goal of studying religions this way would not be to learn about some specified number but to recognize the diversity of religions, as well as the presence of nonbelievers.

Second, it is important that schools not fall into the trap of confusing religious traditions with different kinds of social and political groupings, such as nations or ethnicities. It is common to refer to Muslims as Arabs, Indians as Hindus, or Americans as Christians, but ethnic and political boundaries rarely coincide neatly with religious ones. Using phrases such as "Muslim countries" or "the Muslim world," although common, is highly misleading, because it gives the impression of greater uniformity than actually exists. These phrases not only imply that countries with majority Muslim populations are governed by religious principles (making them "Muslim countries") but also obscures the fact that many millions of Muslims live in countries in which they are minorities, including India, China and the United States. Confusing the distribution of religions with political boundaries leads to a misunderstanding of both politics and religion. When studying any given country, teachers should help students recognize the diversity of religions found there.

Diversity Within Religions

Another important simplification of the "world religions" approach involves portraying each tradition as though all its adherents were fundamentally similar to each other. Although many religions have common beliefs or practices—the five pillars of Islam, veneration of ancestors in Chinese folk religion, monotheism and the Torah in Judaism—religions also are characterized by a great deal of diversity. Judaism, Christianity, Islam and Buddhism, for example, all contain major branches that differ in important ways, and each of these is characterized by further differences among denominations, orders or regional and local traditions. The town I grew up in had only about 2000 inhabitants, yet it was home to seven different Protestant denominations—Baptist, Southern Baptist, Methodist, Presbyterian, Pentecostal, Disciples of Christ and Assembly of God. Even within many denominations, churches and individuals differ in their beliefs and practices. A group such as the Southern Baptists may seem homogeneous to outsiders, and its members are often stereotyped as oppressing women, rejecting science and behaving intolerantly toward other religions. But having grown up in this tradition, I know that it includes an array of social, political and theological perspectives. My high school biology teacher, for example, was also a Southern Baptist Sunday School teacher, and he had no problem reconciling religion and evolution. And far from being intolerant of other religions, the pastor of a Southern Baptist church in a small town once told me, "I know my religion is true. But who am I to say other religions might not also be true? That's not my call."

Most of us know about this diversity in our own religions. Even if some Catholics, Protestants and Orthodox Christians don't know much about the other branches, they at least know they exist; and the members of any given Christian church know that some of their fellow parishioners are either more or less devout than they are. It can be harder, though, to recognize and appreciate diversity in other religions, especially if one's only exposure to them consists of the simplified portraits found in textbooks and mainstream media. Islam, for example, has a wide variety of branches, denominations and traditions, and groups and individuals differ in their ideas about what their faith requires and permits. I know Muslim women who wear niqabs, others who wear hijabs and others who simply dress modestly. I also know Muslims who never drink alcohol, others who drink sparingly and others who don't hesitate to take a drink. Every religion is characterized by such differing interpretations. Thinking that members of a given religion share the same understanding of their faith, or have the same commitment to it, is simply incorrect—particularly when thinking about the millions of followers of the world's largest traditions.

The perception of uniformity is more than incorrect, though; it also has significant consequences for participation in the civic life of a democracy. Drawing conclusions about individuals based on their membership in a given religion is a common but destructive form of stereotyping that misrepresents the lives of many people, both in local communities and around the world, and one that limits students' ability to engage in open-minded deliberation of civic issues. Stereotypes of Muslims as anti-American, much less as terrorists, fail to account for the wide range of attitudes among Muslim American citizens and Muslims in other countries. Certainly none of my many Muslim friends and colleagues—from the United States, Europe, South East Asia, Africa and the Middle East—has ever expressed any support for terrorism, and they are uniformly horrified by such violence. Jews and Catholics have their own long histories with such prejudices.

In John F. Kennedy's 1960 presidential campaign, for example, stereotypes of Catholic uniformity led some detractors to claim that he would be beholden to Vatican policy (Casey, 2009)—an all-too-typical example of judging individuals by supposed group characteristics. Although schools are likely to portray other religions in neutral or positive rather than negative terms, these portrayals are still stereotypes, and lack of attention to diversity within religions reinforces the belief that conclusions can be reached about people by their association with monolithic and essentializing categories. This is a fatal blow to deliberation in civic life: if we think we already know what members of another religion believe, we have no motivation to listen to them or to try to make sense of their arguments.

Recognizing the diversity within religions is also necessary for students to reason independently about their *own* positions on public issues. In some settings, young people face strong pressure to support social and political issues based on their religious identification—good Christians should oppose same-sex marriage, good Muslims should avoid interacting with the opposite sex, good Catholics (in Northern Ireland) should support unification with the Republic. Because religion is so important to many people, these claims can easily trump individual decision-making. If students are deeply committed to their religion, it may seem to them that they have no choice but to follow a given practice or support a particular position—and many political and religious leaders are ready to exploit precisely this perception. Emphasizing the shared characteristics of a religion's followers, without similar attention to their diversity, limits students' ability to understand not only others but themselves.

The alternative to studying simplified depictions of world religions, though, is not to study every difference within each. Few people can develop a deep familiarity with all the variants of their own religion, much less those of others, and attempting such a task in schools is neither realistic nor desirable. There's little enough time to study religions as it is, and trying to cram in dozens of different denominations or variations would lead to the kind of fact-based coverage that doesn't interest students and doesn't expand their understanding. Instead, students need to learn that diversity itself is integral to religion. Students in the middle grades are often asked to create group or individual reports on religions; in doing so, they should focus not only on what members of each religion share with other followers—a short list—but more importantly on what differences characterize that religion. They cannot learn about every variation, but they need to learn that understanding a religion requires investigating its diversity.

Similarly, when considering public issues, students should be encouraged to move beyond misleading simplifications such as "the Christian perspective on abortion" or "the Jewish perspective on Israel" and instead consider the range of ideas people actually hold. Students should know that many Evangelical Christians are more concerned with the environment and income inequality than with abortion and homosexuality; that many Protestants in Northern Ireland work together with Catholics on issues of common concern; that many Muslims are feminists who reject traditional interpretations of gender roles. Only when students are exposed to a range of interpretations grounded in religion can they make informed decisions on their own.

Changes in Religion over Time

A final simplification involves portraying religions as unchanging. Given that studying world religions often takes place within history classes, it is ironic that religions are usually treated so ahistorically. Students may learn about the historical spread of Buddhism, Islam or other religions, as well as the origins of major divisions such as those between Protestant and Catholic Christians, Sunni and Shia Muslims, and Mahayana and Theravada Buddhists. However, they rarely learn about more recent evolutions, or those that occur within major branches. As a result, it is easy to assume that adherents of a religion are little different today than they were hundreds or even thousands of years ago. As recently as the 19th Century, though, many Christians justified slavery on the basis of the Bible; keeping kosher was a cornerstone of Judaism; and Shinto taught that the Japanese emperor was divine. Today, Christians, Jews and Shinto followers can reject these beliefs and still consider themselves devout. As in other areas of social life, religious beliefs and practices change over time.

The perception of continuity over time also has consequences for civic deliberation and decision-making. Citizens can only engage in deliberation if there is something to make a decision *about*; if their choices are forestalled by tradition, then there is no room for maneuver in the present. Yet if religious principles are timeless, then they have to be accepted without modification; true believers must follow the beliefs and practices that have existed since the religion's founding. If religions change over time, on the other hand, then they can still change today; practices that may have seemed logical or served a purpose in the ancient world (or more recently) may be modified as circumstances and social conditions change. Just as students need to see diversity as an essential component of religion, they also need to see change over time as a part of such study.

Students cannot learn about a multitude of religious changes, just as they cannot learn about all their contemporary variations. They can, however, consistently examine such examples so that they come to see change as essential to understanding the topic. As students study a religion, that is, they should identify and investigate some of the changes that have taken place in it over time—not just its historical spread or separation into major branches, but changes in the way its members express their belief and practice. And so that they don't think religious changes only took place long ago, they should also investigate recent and contemporary movements for religious change, which can be found within Christianity, Confucianism, Hinduism, Islam, Judaism and other religions (Aslan, 2011; Cohen & Eisen, 2000; Hefner, 1998; Jenkins, 2011; Tan, 2008; Wilde, 2007).

Avoiding Ethnocentrism in Teaching about Religions

Another problem that plagues the teaching of world religions is ethnocentrism. Sometimes this involves the outright denigration or trivialization of other traditions, but few teachers are as narrow-minded as this, and only overtly sectarian curriculum materials would cast other religions in an unfavorable light. However, other forms of ethnocentrism are subtler, and these affect even educators who work diligently to understand and appreciate religions other than their own. Many religious ideas are so deeply ingrained in our thinking that we don't question their universality, and as a result, we interpret other religions in light of our own backgrounds, despite our desire to do just the opposite.

One common ethnocentric approach emphasizes similarities among religions and treats their differences as matters more of form than substance. This perspective can be especially tempting in light of the prejudice and even violence that often accompanies religious differences. Teaching students that all religions are essentially similar, and that they all reflect humanity's quest for peace, love and spirituality, seems to promote tolerance and mutual respect. However, this ignores very real differences among religions. Although most religions converge around ethical principles, they also display significant differences in their ideas about the nature of the universe and of the place of people and society within it (Prothero, 2010). By ignoring these differences, we fail to help students understand others, and we ultimately sow the seeds of ignorance and mistrust rather than tolerance.

One example of this kind of ethnocentrism involves assuming that all religions have a personal god who knows, loves and cares for humans as individuals. Most versions of Christianity hold that God knows all people personally, intervenes in their lives and listens to their prayers. In some other religions, though, gods are more distant, and their intervention less caring; humans must get their attention, ask for specific favors and provide something in return—a sacrifice or other ritual acknowledgment. In still other religions, deities are even more impersonal and have no ability or desire to intervene in the affairs of humans. Growing up surrounded by one of these traditions makes it hard to understand the others: if gods are impersonal, then talk of love seems misplaced and meaningless; if God is loving, ritual sacrifice seem like childish superstition. This is just one of several differences among religions that stands in the way of mutual understanding.

Exclusivity and Evangelism

Differing ideas about how religions should relate to each other can be particularly difficult to understand. A belief in exclusivity is a core doctrine of Christianity; a believer cannot be both a Christian *and* a member of another religion, and to convert to Christianity means to stop believing in other religions, as the word *conversion* suggests. To some extent, this exclusivity is characteristic of each of the Abrahamic religions. Symbols of other religions are not found in synagogues, churches or mosques, and no one is expected to pray in more than one of these.

Muslims are strongly discouraged from converting to other religions, because by definition that means that they would no longer worship Allah. (Despite such doctrines, though, Christians and Muslims in many parts of the world draw freely from other traditions as part of their belief and practice.)

Yet in Asia—and in communities worldwide with people of Asian ancestry—there is often no pretense of exclusivity, as many individuals practice a combination of religions without feeling obligated to any one in particular. For a time, I was confused by "which religion" certain practices represented (such as burning incense at a small shrine at home or near a workplace), until I learned that these cannot necessarily be categorized as belonging to any single religion. Such practices are *religious*, but they are not thought of as part of *a religion*. Similarly, as I've visited Chinese temples in South East Asia, my friends have explained how some elements within a single site relate to Taoism, some to Buddhism and others to Chinese folk religion—yet there is no sense of contradiction among these. I have also seen many people praying for good fortune at a Buddhist shrine one moment, and then walking next door to pray at a Hindu temple—just to "cover their bases," as one friend puts it. As someone who has grown up in a more exclusive religion, the flexibility and overlap of these beliefs and practices can be hard to understand. My friends, meanwhile, are sometimes baffled by my tendency to sort religious traditions into neat categories.

Related to the idea of exclusivity is that of evangelism. Many Christians believe that anyone who worships other gods (or none) is not only mistaken but faces eternal damnation; logically, then, non-Christians need to be converted for their own sake. Although Christians differ in their commitment to this kind of evangelism, a common practice both today and throughout history is the quest to spread Christianity. This is one reason for tension between Christian and Muslim communities in some parts of the world. Muslim leaders believe—correctly—that Christians actively work to convert their followers. But this missionary zeal is not characteristic of all religions. Although Judaism welcomes new followers, there are no Jewish missionaries, because spreading the word is not part of the religion's practice or belief. Most Hindus, meanwhile, do not even accept the possibility of conversion; only those who are born into the religion can practice it. And the idea of converting to Shinto or Sikhism would simply seem odd, since these are so closely tied to particular locations and ethnicities. Those who grow up in a Christian environment may fail to understand why other religions seem narrowly concerned with their own followers rather than all the world, while those from other backgrounds may not understand why some Christians seem so intent on replacing others' religion with their own.

Belief and Practice

Another pervasive form of ethnocentrism involves giving primary attention to beliefs, as found in scripture and formal doctrine. This is a natural emphasis for educators raised within Abrahamic traditions, because belief is central to Judaism, Christianity and Islam, and each relies on a set of scriptures. Christians, for example, are "saved" by their belief that Jesus died to redeem them from sin; similarly, the first pillar of Islam is the profession that there is no God but Allah, and that Mohammed is his prophet. In both cases, belonging is defined by belief, and members of these religions are often called "believers." Each of the Abrahamic religions also has a long tradition of formal theology, in which scholars over the ages have systematized the meaning and consequences of founding scriptures. Studying other religions would seem to require a similar familiarity with the central beliefs of each.

For many years, I tried to understand the beliefs of other religions, and I was disappointed that this was so hard to do. I knew the basic principles of Judaism, Christianity and Islam, and I could see how these influence the lives of Jews, Christians and Muslims. So why did I have trouble seeing the same connections in other religions, even after reading about them repeatedly and visiting places of worship? I finally realized that not all religions are so concerned with codified systems of belief. As a friend in Singapore explained while showing me around a Hindu temple, there is no theology or founding scripture of Hinduism; it includes a wide variety of prescriptions and philosophies from different cultures and traditions, and its followers do not universally subscribe to any single belief. To characterize it as a belief system is not only misleading but also unwieldy, because no one can become familiar with all the strands of thought within Hinduism (much less middle schoolers studying it for a week). Similarly, my experiences in South East Asia helped me see that Chinese folk religion is impossible to define in terms of systematic belief, much less of theology. It involves the veneration of a diverse array of spirits—ancestors, nature deities, cultural heroes, historical figures, and others—and these vary across villages, provinces and countries. Nowhere are its traditions set down in a single, authoritative set of scriptures, nor could they be.

Buddhism, on the other hand, does seem to have a coherent system of beliefs, based on the teachings of its founder. Like many middle and high school students, somewhere along the way I learned about Buddhist concepts such as the Middle Way, the Four Noble Truths and the Eightfold Path. I also learned that Buddhism is more a philosophy than a system of worship: followers venerate the Buddha as an enlightened teacher, but they don't think of him as a god, nor do they pray to him. But then, like many Americans who travel to Asia, I was shocked to see many Buddhists doing just that: worshipping statues of Buddha and praying to him for good fortune. Formal Buddhist teachings have little connection to the practice of many Buddhists, who may not even be very familiar with the religion's philosophical components.

In each of these examples, problems arise when we think of formal belief as the defining characteristic of a religion. Although members of every religion have beliefs, those are not always systematic or widely shared; even more important, they are not always key to defining what the religion means to its adherents. Understanding a religion requires paying attention to the variety of ways that people engage with it, including the *scriptural* (the composition and use of religious texts), the *personal* (individuals' quest to cultivate and transform themselves), the *liturgical* (procedures conducted by priests, monks or other ritual specialists), the *practical* (looking for immediate results using religious techniques) and the *relational* (relations among humans, deities and ancestors) (Chau, 2006; Palmer, Shive, & Wickeri, 2011). Religions differ greatly in which of these its adherents consider most important, and this is an essential understanding for students to develop: they need to understand what aspects of religion are important to *others*, rather than thinking that members of each distribute their attention in the same way.

Overcoming Ethnocentrism

Ethnocentrism is difficult to overcome. Its very pervasiveness makes it tricky to identify, and we often employ the limited perspectives of our own religious backgrounds without realizing it. This is why reading or formal study does not necessarily broaden our understanding: we interpret what we read through our own lenses, and if the authors we read come from backgrounds like our own, they may already have engaged in similar interpretations. Works by members of other religions, meanwhile, often present idealistic portrayals, which sometimes are geared precisely toward the preconceptions of others. It is not easy to understand the role that religion plays in the lives of people from other backgrounds.

There is no magic remedy for this situation. My own experience, however, suggests one possible path for better understanding. Over the course of many years, I read summary after summary of Hinduism, yet I never felt that I understood it, and I couldn't even retain most of the information I came across. When I began traveling to Asia, I always made it a point to visit Hindu temples, but still I felt I had little idea what the religion was about. But when a Hindu colleague took me to his temple, and later to a community festival, I felt I learned more about the beliefs and practices of Hinduism than I ever had before. He didn't try to provide an authoritative and public account of Hinduism, only to tell me what it involved for people in his community. I could ask him questions that weren't easily answered by texts or temples—not only philosophical questions but very practical ones, like, "Why are those people cutting open coconuts?" From him, I had an insider's perspective, and one that I could understand. It was still only one person's viewpoint, of course, but this personal view was more comprehensible than anything I had before.

This experience has led me to reflect on the broader issue of overcoming religious ethnocentrism. Most of what I know about the meaning and practice of Judaism, Islam and Taoism comes from *people*—my Jewish, Muslim and Taoist friends. This learning usually happens not during a discussion of religion itself but simply in the course of daily life—a Jewish colleague who needs me to buy him a drink because he can't carry a wallet on the Sabbath, a Muslim student who tells me about buying hijabs as fashion accessories, Taoist-influenced colleagues who warn me not to eat fried foods when I have a cold. Even much of what I know about Christianity has come from those I grew up with. Other people "know" what Evangelical Christians are like from hearing about them in the media. I know about them from seeing my Sunday School teacher send get-well and sympathy cards on behalf of her Sunday School class; from watching businesspeople in my hometown treat their customers fairly; from listening to gossip in the vestibule. Conversations and personal connections are far more effective at conveying insiders' perspectives on religious belief and practice than formal descriptions or scripture. The most effective remedy to ethnocentrism is talking with people and spending time with them.

Not everyone, though, is fortunate enough to have so many friends from other backgrounds. In the absence of opportunities for direct conversation, two other sources can convey authentic voices to teachers and their students. The first of these is literature—short stories, novels, memoirs and biographies from the perspective of members of different religions. The most effective of such sources are not those that are *about* a given religion, because those can present narrow or prescribed ideals. More effective are engaging stories about the hopes, dreams and struggles of three-dimensional people in the recent past or contemporary world. This kind of literature helps students see the role of religion in everyday life and its significance for its adherents. (Suggestions can be found in sources such as Khan, n.d.; Silver, 2010; and Smith, 2012.) A second source for such voices is the Internet. Internet resources can be chaotic, offensive, extremist and inaccurate—but they can also provide engaging, authentic and touching insights to which teachers and students would otherwise have little access. A series of videos of Muslim women in seven countries explaining why they do or do not wear hijabs (Radio Free Europe/Radio Liberty, 2014), for example, provides voices that many students would not otherwise hear.

Social, Political and Psychological Dimensions of Religion

Although students often study *religions*, they rarely learn about the social, political or psychological dimensions of *religion*. That is, they study some of the religions that exist, but they have few opportunities to consider what religion means for individual identity or in society at large. They may touch on this topic in specialized courses in sociology or psychology at the senior high level, but even advanced government courses are unlikely to help students understand the political use of religion. Instead, religion is often treated as a force to be considered but not analyzed: students learn that religion influences some people's political decisions, but they do not delve into why religion is such a powerful force. The relation between religion and politics is treated as though it is both self-evident and inevitable.

This lack of attention to the social, political and psychological meanings of religion leaves students unprepared to understand important aspects of social life. Without learning about the political context of religion, for example, students cannot understand many of the conflicts that beset the world today and have throughout history. At the time of this writing, Buddhists have been killing Muslims in Myanmar; Hindus have been killing Muslims in India; Muslims have been killing Christians in Pakistan; Sunnis and Shias have been killing each other in Iraq; and Christians and Muslims have been killing each other in Nigeria and the Central African Republic. By the time this chapter is published, new religious hostilities will have arisen in one part of the world or another, and less extreme—but still troubling—conflicts are likely to have persisted: violence between Protestants and Catholics in Northern Ireland, desecration of Jewish temples and cemeteries in western Europe, discrimination against Buddhists in Tibet and Shias in Malaysia. Historical examples are all too easy to add to the list: centuries of pogroms against Jews, the Hindu–Muslim violence that accompanied the partition of India and Pakistan, mob attacks on Mormons in the 19th-Century United States, the Thirty Years War in 17th-Century Europe, and on and on and on.

Studying the beliefs and practices of world religions without analyzing their societal context fails to help students make sense of such conflicts. None of these problems results directly from differences in belief or practice. After all, Catholics and Protestants are members of the same religion, and there are relatively few differences in their beliefs; the same can be said of Sunnis and Shias. To think that religious conflicts result directly from differences of faith is to oversimplify and misunderstand their causes. Worse, it gives the impression that religious tension is inevitable, as though members of different religions—or even denominations—who live near each other must always be at each other's throats.

Violent and enduring conflicts usually have causes that extend beyond differences in religious belief and practice; those differences become a way of expressing political and economic tensions, or a means by which support is mobilized for political ends. Sometimes, these tensions are over material resources. Throughout history, religious violence has often been an expression of territorial disputes; when groups that compete for the same land, water or other resource also adhere to different traditions, the dispute appears to be about religion rather than territory. Other times, religion is invoked as a path to political power, as leaders and would-be leaders seek to gain support by drawing on religious passions. Religious violence, that is, does not simply "break out"; rather, religion is manipulated to serve other purposes. Individuals and communities of different faiths often have lived next to each other peacefully and productively for decades or centuries before their differences become exploited for political ends, and bloodshed results. In order to understand religion, students need to examine this process, or they may misinterpret religion as an inevitable source of discord.

Students also need to understand that the political use of religion is not limited to other countries, the distant past or situations of violence or extreme persecution. Religion is also highly politicized in the United States and other established democracies. In Europe, for example, right-wing political parties have recently garnered support by vilifying non-Christian immigrants and portraying their dress, dietary regulations and social norms as a threat to national culture. In the United States, politicians often call attention to issues with a religious dimension and then portray themselves—implicitly or explicitly—as the voice of conservative Christian beliefs. One of the clearest examples of this came in 2004, when proposed amendments to bar same-sex marriage were placed on the ballots of eleven states in the hope of increasing the turnout of socially conservative voters (Smith, SeSantis, & Kassel, 2006). Opposition to same-sex marriage did not spontaneously arise in this case any more than religious violence "breaks out" in communities where people of differing faiths have lived together for many years. Rather, religion was manipulated for political ends.

Religion is not only used for nefarious purposes, though: it has also been the foundation for altruistic and liberating movements throughout history. The abolitionist movement in Britain and the United States, for example, was rooted in two religious traditions—Quakerism's radical egalitarianism and Evangelicalism's emphasis on conscience and individual moral choice (Stewart, 1997). Similarly, the U.S. Civil Rights movement drew much of its strength from the theology of Christianity and the organizational capacity of African American churches (Taylor, 2002). And Buddhist religious leaders have been a source of opposition to repressive political regimes in countries such as Myanmar, Tibet and Vietnam. In these cases, too, religion has been used for political purposes—not in order to slaughter others, but to stand up for them, often at great cost to those who do so.

How can religious beliefs be so easily mobilized for political purposes, whether good or ill? What is it about religion that leads people either to attack their neighbors or to risk their own well-being for them? Knowing about the beliefs and practices of world religions does little to help students answer this. In order to understand the political uses of religion, students must also understand its social and psychological dimensions—how it provides emotional and material support, creates a sense of identity and gives meaning to people's lives. Religion is useful politically only because it plays such a positive and pervasive role in the lives of so many individuals and communities. This is important for all students to recognize, but it may be especially important for those who do not consider themselves religious. For them, the motivating power of religion can seem foreign, even irrational; it's hard to see how beliefs they consider nothing more than superstitions can influence people's behavior in such remarkable ways.

Although many of the topics mentioned above—such as connections between religious movements and political developments—are easiest to imagine in social studies classes in middle or high school, the social and psychological aspects of religion are something that students can investigate from the primary grades onward, even though they rarely do so. Of course, primary students will not be studying the philosophical or sociological foundations of religion, at least not using those terms. But they can learn how religion is involved in major life events—birth, marriage and death—as well as the daily, weekly and annual religious practices in which many people take part. A number of books for primary students introduce such topics, including *Birth Customs* (Rushton, 1993a), *Initiation Customs* (Prior, 1993a), *Festivals* (Livingston, 1996), *Food and Fasting* (Burke, 1993), *Marriage Customs* (Compton, 1993), *Pilgrimages and Journeys* (Prior, 1993b), *Death Customs* (Rushton, 1993b), and *Why do We Celebrate That?* (Wilcox, 1996). Many students will also be able to draw upon their own experiences, because families often include children in religious ceremonies and celebrations from an early age.

The purpose of studying religion in this way obviously is not to inculcate religious belief, but it is also not necessarily to teach about the practices of any particular religion. Rather, it is to help students understand how religion *in general* affects people's lives and why it's important to them. Knowing the specific devotional practices of Muslims or Buddhists, or knowing the particular marriage rituals found in Christianity or Hinduism, is not particularly important. But knowing that many people worship daily or weekly, or that when people get married they often do so in religious settings, is fundamental to understanding why so many people care about religion.

Students in the upper elementary grades and beyond can investigate an even wider variety of roles for religion in the lives of individuals and communities. Religion does not only form the setting for worship and celebration; it also provides a context for socializing and for sharing resources, both through organized charity and small-scale efforts to support those in need. By interviewing family members or others, students can learn about how people are involved in religious communities and what influence those communities have on them. Students can also explore the psychological dimensions of religion through literature in which characters struggle with its personal and social demands. (See suggestions in Carnegie Library of Pittsburg, 2013.)

Conclusions

As many educators have argued, expanding religion's place in the curriculum may enhance students' understanding of individuals and society, as well as their ability to participate more meaningfully in the public life of a pluralist, democratic society. Achieving these goals requires more than increasing the amount of time and space given to the topic, however; it means reconsidering how we teach about religion. Covering basic facts about the beliefs of selected world religions is not adequate for understanding such a complex feature of human life, and portraying all religions as similar does little to help students understand the perspectives of others. Rather than simply including more content about religions, schools need to provide a more comprehensive way of making sense both of individual religions and the role of religion in social life. These include attention to the range of religious beliefs and practices locally and throughout t of undergraduate teacher education students' heavily Christian understandings of their "calling" and purpose as future teachers. This would not be an easy sample set to find at the University of *Washington*. Still, it might hold interest for the Christians among us, even those who would be wary of teachers who speak more about "loving kids" than intellectually forming them.

*Per above, the notion of "calling" can be a very powerful concept for teachers of faith, and there also might be non-Christian appropriations of that term or other valuable terms that get at the same idea. It would be interesting to hear one another's notions about a "call to teach" (or counsel, or administrate!).

*The Schweber (religion's impact on students' learning), Barton (religion's role in the curriculum), and Kunzman (managing "certainty" in ethical dialogue) chapters of the book are all excellent in my view, and feel free to draw upon one or the other in your response. Regarding the Kunzman chapter, some might feel that ethical or religious certainty is attainable. A better view might be that no one is certain of anything, but that faith does call us to 'lean in' as much as possible to our views of the world. This posture maintains both intellectual/spiritual humility and commitment.

[Handwritten annotations:]

Extreme-spectrum

Help others

- History
- social studies
- Literature/L.A.

Reply:

Pg 56 - Manage students' → surface the issue

Pg 58² - Private v. civic
↳ God parents participate in kids' school
↳ No such experiment

Pg 73-74
① Using each to teach religion
(Turn literature
② Other facets of religion
social, polit., philosoph., psych.

Pg 30
multiple religions

Pg 64 - How to teach religion? not just
might own
not conforming
not unchanging

Pg 72 - Religion/practices not cleanest

Moderns v. deist discussion → 3 major faiths
→ NO celebrate
→ NO non atheist

significance
(why does that
takes more

have to do w/
religion?

Mormon

goes to church
don't drink

Pg XII

Why? 1) Encompasses - presence a theme
2) Elephant in the room - need to be examined.

Pg 4: Diff → then talk (Chiship) student → more
replic fundamentalist views

Pg 5 Ideological homogenous communities
Multiplying → democratic education
minority strong foundation

Pg 8
P 10 - Think of Montessori

My upbringing Plural
- Part of life / religious
not preaching!
dont study texts

[handwritten: Mindful, intentional and be able to accept enthusiasm deal w/ it/empathically]

Religion in the Classroom: Dilemmas for Democratic Education (James, with Schweber, Kunzman, Barton, and Logan chapters, 2015)

*This text adds another topic to Routledge's series on democratic education and teaching, which Greg has pitched as a worthy conceptual umbrella for thinking morally about popular education (public and private, though the majority of children attend public schools), after exploring Catholic and Protestant ideas about faith and morality in general in our first two books.

*Educational practitioners might find Ch. 3 especially useful, James' primer on the "establishment of religion" and "freedom of religion" clauses of the 1st Amendment to the Constitution, and the "Lemon" and "Sherbert" tests, among other significant guidelines and interpretations. James is not a legal scholar and Greg can direct you to fuller treatments, but James is right that knowing this basic terrain is incredibly important for teaching in diverse contexts. *[handwritten: Gray areas / 1st amendment]*

[handwritten margin notes: 3 rule 9/16, clauses, Establishment → intention is key, Exercise, Exercise]

*One *critical* fact in processing James' thinking about the background privileging of Christianity in public schools - e.g. the calendar, or disproportionate use of Christian sources for celebrating the winter holidays, or even in some cases outright prayers and the displaying of Christian symbols - is that she's writing from *Georgia*, part of the more traditional American south. **You might feel this is an important reminder of the privileging of mainstream culture in our Pacific Northwest, specifically the greater Seattle area, but you might also feel that almost the opposite is the actual situation here. It would be interesting to hear your perceptions on this.** *[handwritten: Dominant Class, celebrate all holidays]*

[handwritten margin notes: By, Norman]

*This same geographic and demographic issue might inform James's discussion of [...]

the world; the diversity found within religions, and their change over time; the meaning that religions hold for individuals beyond doctrine and scripture; and the social, political and psychological uses of religion. Significant obstacles stand in the way of implementing this vision of teaching about religion, but anything less is likely to perpetuate ignorance and misunderstanding rather than overcome it.

References

Aslan, R. (2011). *No god but God: The origins, evolution, and future of Islam* (updated ed.). New York: Random House.

Burke, D. (1993). *Food and fasting*. New York: Thomson Learning.

Carnegie Library of Pittsburg. (2013). *Believers and doubters: Teen fiction about religion*. http://www.carnegielibrary.org/teens/books/showbooklist.cfm?catid=6&list=spirituality

Casey, S. (2009). *The making of a Catholic president: Kennedy vs. Nixon, 1960*. New York: Oxford University Press.

Chau, A.Y. (2006). *Miraculous response: Doing popular religion in contemporary China*. Stanford, CA: Stanford University Press.

Chinese Folk Religion Adherents by Country. (2011). Chartsbin. http://chartsbin.com/view/sgx

Cohen, S.M., & Eisen, A.M. (2000). *The Jew within: Self, family, and community in America*. Bloomington, IN: Indiana University Press.

Compton, A. (1993). *Marriage customs*. New York: Thomson Learning.

Hefner, R.W. (1998). Multiple modernities: Christianity, Islam, and Hinduism in a globalizing age. *Annual Review of Anthropology, 27*, 83–104.

Goossaert, V. (2005). Chinese religion: Popular religion. In L. Jones (Ed.), *Encyclopedia of religion*, vol. 3 (2nd ed.) (pp. 1613–1621). Detroit, MI: Macmillan Reference USA.

Green, C.R., & Oldendorf, S.B. (2011). *Religious diversity and children's literature: Strategies and resources*. Charlotte, NC: Information Age Publishing.

Jenkins, P. (2011). *The next Christendom: The coming of global Christianity* (3rd ed.). New York: Oxford University Press.

Khan, R. (n.d.) *Children's books with Muslim and related cultural themes*. http://www.rukhsanakhan.com/muslimbooklist/Muslimbooklist.pdf

Livingston, M.C. (1996). *Festivals*. New York: Holiday House.

Nash, R.J., & Bishop, P.A. (2010). *Teaching adolescents religious literacy in a post-9/11 world*. Charlotte, NC: Information Age Publishing.

Nord, W.A. (1995). *Religion and American education: Rethinking a national dilemma*. Chapel Hill, NC: University of North Carolina Press.

Nord, W.A., & Haynes, C.C. (1998). *Taking religion seriously across the curriculum*. Alexandria, VA: Association for Supervision and Curriculum Development.

Palmer, D.A., Shive, G., & Wickeri, P.L. (2011). *Chinese religious life*. New York: Oxford University Press.

Prior, K. (1993a). *Initiation customs*. New York: Thomson Learning.

Prior, K. (1993b). *Pilgrimages and journeys*. New York: Thomson Learning.

Prothero, S. (2010). *God is not one: The eight rival religions that run the world—and why their differences matter*. New York: HarperOne.

Radio Free Europe/Radio Liberty. (2014). *Project Hijab*. http://www.rferl.org/media/video/Project_Hijab/2126184.html?z=3248&zp=1

Rushton, L. (1993a). *Birth customs*. New York: Thomson Learning.

Rushton, L. (1993b). *Death customs*. New York: Thomson Learning.

Secular/Nonreligious/Agnostic/Atheist. (2013). World Religions Ranked by Adherents. http://www.adherents.com/Religions_By_Adherents.html#Nonreligious

Silver, L.R. (2010). *Best Jewish books for children and teens*. Philadelphia, PA: Jewish Publication Society.

Smith, C.L. (2012). *Children's and YA books with Asian heritage themes*. http://www.cynthia leitichsmith.com/lit_resources/diversity/asian_am/asian_am.html

Smith, D.A., SeSantis, M., & Kassel, J. (2006). Same-sex marriage ballot measures and the 2004 presidential election. *State and Local Government Review, 38*, 78–91.

Stewart, J.B. (1997). *Holy warriors: The abolitionists and American slavery* (rev. ed.). New York: Hill and Wang.

Susskind, Y. (2007). Honor killings in the new Iraq: The murder of Du'a Aswad. *Counterpunch*, May 17, 2007. http://www.counterpunch.org/2007/05/17/the-murder-of-du-a-aswad/

Tan, S.-H. (2008). Modernizing Confucianism and "new Confucianism." In K. Louie (Ed.), *The Cambridge companion to modern Chinese culture* (pp. 135–155). New York: Cambridge University Press.

Taylor, C. (2002). *Black religious intellectuals: The fight for equality from Jim Crow to the 21st century*. New York: Routledge.

Terman, R.L. (2010). To specify or single out: Should we use the term "honor killing"? *Muslim World Journal of Human Rights, 7*(1), Article 2.

Wilcox, J. (1996). *Why do we celebrate that?* New York: Holiday House.

Wilde, M.J. (2007). *Vatican II: A sociological study of religious change*. Princeton, NJ: Princeton University Press.

8

TALKING WITH STUDENTS WHO ALREADY KNOW THE ANSWER

Navigating Ethical Certainty in Democratic Dialogue

Robert Kunzman

Guiding Questions:

In what ways does ethical certainty get in the way of democratic dialogue?
How might we help students to navigate religiously infused ethical dialogue?

"God says it, I believe it, and that settles it." So goes the refrain of a once-popular Christian gospel song, a sentiment that resonates with many conservative Christians who view biblical scripture as the blueprint for the values, priorities and decisions that shape their lives. Plenty of people across many religious traditions—and no religion at all—hold fast to certain ethical commitments that they view as absolute and non-negotiable. My intent in this chapter is not to criticize such steadfastness as something to be avoided, but rather to suggest ways that teachers can help students navigate the tension that exists between ethical certainty and democratic dialogue. When citizens engage in dialogue and deliberation with the goal of making rules about the shape and norms of our public life together, they quite reasonably expect a degree of open-mindedness from their fellow citizens, a willingness to consider values and perspectives beyond their own. Ethical certainty complicates this endeavor.

This chapter explores the challenges and opportunities of helping students learn how to engage respectfully and productively with ethical difference in the public school setting, particularly when such difference is informed by religious certainty—a conviction that their beliefs are beyond the possibility of error. My particular focus here will be conservative Christian students, for two primary reasons: first, despite the growing religious diversity of the United States, about three-quarters of the population still identify as Christian, with perhaps one-third of that group constituting theological conservatives, Evangelicals, or fundamentalists[1]

(Gallup, 2012; Pew, 2012). Second, conservative Christians often bring a degree of certainty—drawn from their interpretation of God's will through biblical scripture and church teachings—that complicates possibilities of genuine dialogue with fellow citizens as they attempt to navigate their religious and ethical differences.

Despite my focus here on conservative Christians, and this book's broader focus on religion in education, it is important to recognize that the deliberative obligations of democratic citizenship require thoughtful engagement with a broad array of values and priorities. We cannot judge fairly among competing visions of the good society—and the laws and policies that come with such visions—if we are not willing to listen carefully to our fellow citizens about what matters to them and why.

These values are typically more than just a sense of right and wrong; they emerge from our particular vision of the good life. This may not be a singular model (many believe that good lives can take a variety of forms), but most of us have a sense of what we value and why. This broader realm—not just "what is it good to *do*?" but also "who is it good to *be*?"—is what the ancient Greek philosophers termed *ethics* (Williams, 1985).

Clearly, our ethical perspectives are not always informed by religion; these fundamental conceptions of value and purpose can be shaped by a variety of cultural sources and personal experiences. Regardless of their sources, they orient us toward a particular conception of what it means to live well, and this in turn informs our perspective on how society should be structured to enable such lives. Advocating for schools that help students learn to dialogue across ethical difference, then, does not inherently privilege religious value systems—we all draw from ethical sources to guide our vision of what it means to live a good life, and we need to learn how to talk with our fellow citizens when those visions conflict.

We also know from experience that ethical certainty is not solely a byproduct of religious sources—plenty of non-religious people assert that certain actions or ways of life are indisputably right or wrong, good or bad. That being said, it seems that religion might be a special case, perhaps not of kind, but of intensity. For fervent believers, religion is often inextricably woven into their identity. Asking students to consider the possibility that their religiously informed view on a controversial issue might be wrong could be experienced by them as an attack on the ethical framework that gives fundamental meaning and purpose to their lives.

The presence of religion in democratic dialogue creates other potential complications as well. Philosopher Richard Rorty (1999) labels religion a conversation-stopper, claiming that when citizens point to religious scripture or the will of God as the reason for their political positions, there's nothing left to talk about—they've entered the realm of incommensurable criteria, with no way to judge among claims. And just as daunting, participants who are antagonistic toward religion may reject out of hand any assertion or perspective stemming from religious sources, sometimes resorting to caricature or oversimplification.

Many democratic theorists (e.g. Rawls, 1999; Audi, 2000) conclude that the only way to escape this thicket is to keep religion out of our political conversations and decisions about public policy.[2] Religious convictions are viewed as private matters that only merit inclusion in democratic dialogue if they can be translated into arguments that don't rely on religious rationales; offering reasons that non-religious citizens can't accept is seen as disrespectful.

But other theorists find this approach overly restrictive. Jeffrey Stout (2004) contends that limiting our democratic conversations to reasons that we can share in common is unrealistic, and can sometimes force religious participants to be disingenuous about their motivations. Furthermore, Stout questions whether offering religious reasons is in fact inherently disrespectful. If we explain why we support or reject a certain policy based on deeply held religious reasons, we can still follow that with genuine conversation that seeks to understand other perspectives, engages thoughtfully with objections raised, and strives to show our fellow citizens how their arguments are not as compelling as our own. The presence of religiously informed arguments should be taken as a sign of forthright engagement rather than disrespectful manipulation.

Stout and others (e.g. Allen, 2004) caution against the reification of "ideal speech" rules to be applied in all democratic dialogues, where abstract, analytical reasoning is privileged. There are times when the power of emotional appeals, and the telling of compelling stories, generate greater understanding and insight than propositional assertions can muster. Setting up restrictions ahead of time for the kinds of arguments, and the styles of communication employed, not only unfairly empowers some participants more than others, but also unhelpfully limits opportunities for understanding across unfamiliar perspectives. When Martin Luther King, Jr. employed rhetorical devices (e.g. the repetition of "I have a dream") or emotionally evocative language (calling actions "sinful" instead of merely "wrong"), he was connecting to his audience in a way that abstract arguments alone could not. But King's messages did not forgo empirical data and logical analysis either—it was the combination that communicated most effectively and clearly his perspective. With this in mind, then, Stout and other like-minded theorists advocate a more improvisational approach to democratic dialogue, wherein different kinds of arguments and reasons are used depending on the context, the participants and the goals.

Vital Conceptual Distinctions

This improvisational approach to democratic dialogue holds profound educational implications. The less that democratic dialogue relies on procedures and rules, and the more it relies on the judgment and skill of participants, then the greater the importance of citizens gaining insight and experience in talking across ethical differences—particularly when religion is involved. Helping students to learn and employ practical dialogical strategies such as active listening is important, but I want to suggest that cultivating clarity regarding key dialogical concepts is a vital prerequisite to effective use of those conversational skills.

With this in mind, I offer four conceptual distinctions that are crucial in helping students to navigate religiously informed ethical disagreement. They are:

- Respect requires understanding but not endorsement.
- Recognizing the difference between public and private realms creates space and security for private beliefs.
- Civic humility doesn't require ethical relativism or revision of core beliefs.
- Civic deliberation doesn't require consensus, but rather continued conversation.

Respect Requires Understanding but not Endorsement

Probably the most common theme of all classroom rules, respect carries a variety of meanings. In the context of civic dialogue amidst ethical disagreement, students need to gain clarity about what respect requires (understanding) and what it doesn't require (endorsement). We demonstrate civic respect toward others not by agreeing with them, but by striving mightily to understand what they value and why.

Note how respect makes different demands on us than tolerance. We can tolerate other visions of the good life without making any effort to understand those values and commitments—providing opportunities for students and employees to be absent for their major religious holidays, for example. And sometimes a "live and let live" approach to public life is an effective one. But there will be many times when ethical values and commitments will be incompatible: we cannot fully honor a citizen's belief that harvesting embryonic stems cells is akin to murder, for instance, while also permitting other citizens to pursue their conviction that such research is both moral and vital. Similarly, we cannot insist on a zero-tolerance policy for weapons at school while also allowing Sikh boys to wear ceremonial daggers to school.

In those cases, when conflicting ethical values result in at least one set of commitments not being affirmed in public policy, respect plays a vital role. Disrespect occurs when we seek to use the power of the state to restrict others' enactment of their vision of the good life, without understanding the significance of those beliefs. The kind of understanding that citizens need to cultivate amidst ethical disagreement extends beyond mere propositional knowledge. Respect requires us to make sincere, repeated efforts to engage imaginatively with unfamiliar ethical perspectives—not only what others believe, but *why* they believe it (Kunzman, 2006). For example, it's not enough to acknowledge that the Sikh religion requires males to wear the Kirpan or even to know its historical origin as a weapon; we must strive to understand its centrality to the identity and honor of Sikh males as something well beyond a symbolic weapon.

There will certainly be times, however, when substantive understanding of a fellow citizen's ethical perspective will not generate acceptance or endorsement of that perspective. Gaining a nuanced appreciation for the ways that some traditional patriarchal cultures seek to honor women even while tightly circumscribing their potential life options, for instance, would almost certainly not lead public school officials to endorse such limitations in the curricular offerings available to girls at school. Such a refusal does not constitute disrespect, but rather informed disagreement.

Learning how to demonstrate respect through substantive understanding is a demanding yet vital task. It requires a willingness to move beyond simply knowing about something or someone, to an imaginative engagement that has the potential to influence our understanding of the world. Teachers will often need to help their students move past the colloquial conception of respect as acceptance; doing so may ease resistance from students (and their parents) and help them explore and engage with unfamiliar values and traditions more freely.

Recognizing the Difference between Public and Private Realms Creates Space and Security for Private Beliefs

The health of a liberal democracy depends upon its people identifying with the role of democratic citizenship, and exercising its rights and responsibilities. But all of us have additional, private identities and obligations that are at least as important to us—family, cultural community and oftentimes religion. Recognizing the distinction between these public and private realms (what I term *realm recognition*) is a crucial task for democratic education.

Students need to understand that citizens cannot expect—nor should they seek—a society that is a mirror image of their private ethical convictions. Realm recognition can be defended from both a principled and practical perspective. Most religious adherents in the United States do not seek a theocracy where religious leaders run the government and religious law replaces civil law. For all but the most extreme fundamentalist Christians, such an arrangement can be critiqued on theological grounds, emerging either from a belief that political power corrupts faith or from a respect for individual freedom and will. Such a critique is a good example of immanent criticism, a potentially valuable approach that engages religious traditions on their own terms, so to speak, employing their assumptions and assertions to provide an internal analysis or critique.[3]

But a compelling *practical* case can be also made for the importance of realm recognition. A lack of distinction between private and public poses as many risks for the religious believer as anyone else, since there is no guarantee that her religion would retain power—and even if it did, internal disagreements might one day result in her being labeled a heretic and thus an enemy of the state. Democracy is the imperfect compromise that seeks room for disagreement among ethical traditions, in part by preserving a civic realm distinct from private beliefs

(Kunzman, 2011). This means that the public realm will never fully reflect our private ethical commitments—and this disjunction serves as evidence that space remains available in the private realm for differing visions of the good life to be pursued and realized.

The challenging question, of course, is how the two realms should relate to each other, how we should express our private convictions in the public square— perhaps even with the goal of influencing the shape of that realm. While people live the bulk of their lives in the private realm guided by their own visions of the good life, mutual respect requires a different sort of conversation when we're deciding how we will live together. As noted earlier, this distinction between public and private realms, and the need to communicate differently in them, is not about the prohibition of religious perspectives in civic deliberation. Rather, it's a recognition that different contexts require different approaches, and that when we're advocating for decisions that will affect the lives of others, we should exercise what Christopher Eberle (2002, p. 104) calls "conscientious engagement"— striving to frame our deeply held convictions in ways that will resonate with our conversational partners. One vital ingredient in these conversations is civic humility.

Civic Humility Doesn't Require Ethical Relativism or Revision of Core Beliefs

How can we have respectful and productive dialogue with religious citizens who seem so certain about their own positions, who appear unwilling to acknowledge that their ethical convictions might be mistaken? The intensity of ethical certainty that some conservative Christians bring to democratic dialogue in the classroom can make teachers reluctant to encourage such conversational engagement (James, 2010). Depending upon the classroom context and pedagogical goals, however, there may be more room for passionate conviction and productive dialogue to coexist than appears on the surface.

Respectful deliberation across ethical disagreement requires some degree of open-mindedness, a civic humility that entails a willingness to consider alternative perspectives and how those views should influence our decisions. The question is: how much open-mindedness, and open-mindedness about what? Many of our deeply held identities and commitments will be private ones (religious or otherwise) that are, necessarily and quite appropriately, close-minded and not readily open to revision. What matters most to us about who we are and what we believe is not continually "up for grabs."

But civic humility remains a realizable virtue because of the principle of realm recognition. Civic deliberation is intended to help us reach decisions about the shape of our life together in the public realm; the humility and open-mindedness required here involve public policy, not private beliefs. Put another way, civic humility doesn't demand we continually reconsider our private ethical identities and commitments, particularly those of a foundational nature such as belief in God. What civic humility does require, however, is a sense of fallibilism about the application of our private beliefs to our shared laws and public policy (Kunzman, 2011).

There are at least three very practical reasons for avoiding intentional critique of core religious beliefs themselves as part of the public school curriculum. First, most teachers will not have the academic background necessary for such a theological analysis. Second, the compulsory nature of public schooling requires that teachers tread carefully when it comes to the religious beliefs of their students.[4] Third, deliberation about such theological topics tends to distract from civic matters and typically affords no resolution; with this in mind, Hand and Levinson (2012) caution against classroom discussions that reduce "a wide range of interesting and complex ethical disagreements to a single and intractable disagreement about the existence of God" (pp. 625–626). Liberal democracies need citizens who can acknowledge such a theistic starting point among their fellow citizens, and still engage in productive and respective deliberation about societal rules and boundaries.

At the outset of this chapter, I made the case for an improvisational approach to democratic dialogue, one without strict exclusions of religious language and reasoning. Such conversational flexibility not only acknowledges citizens in their ethical particularities, but provides broader possibilities for understanding and insight. As Paul Weithman (2002) observes, religious traditions can sometimes provide reasons and even language—such as arguments against discrimination during the Civil Rights movement—that force citizens to understand issues in starkly moral terms. At the same time, however, the appropriateness and impact of reasons will certainly vary by context and purpose. If we want to persuade someone who does not accept the reasons we give (such as when they are derived from religious scripture), we need to find additional reasons. Civic humility includes such a recognition of context and purpose.[5]

While the principle of realm recognition should make civic humility a more tenable virtue for religious citizens, it does not—and cannot—construct an impermeable barrier that prevents students from ever shifting their core ethical convictions. Seeking to understand holds open the possibility of being changed, and anyone who genuinely engages with the beliefs and perspectives of others stands to be influenced by them. Ethical revision is certainly a real possibility amidst an education that exposes students to art, literature, science—any rich exploration of the world and humanity's place in it. But for the purposes of democratic dialogue, ethical revision of private ethical identities, values and commitments should not be the primary goal.

Civic humility requires, and enables, a necessary open-mindedness about the shape of our public life together. At the same time, its bounded nature can also provide substantive distance between civic obligations and private commitments, and thus offer a way for religious citizens to engage in democratic dialogue.

Civic Deliberation Doesn't Require Consensus, but Rather Continued Conversation

In a liberal democracy, citizens engage in deliberation as part of making decisions about the laws and policies that govern our civic lives. Ideally, this decision reflects a consensus or compromise among conflicting perspectives, but often this will not be the case. Frequently, there will be winners and losers. To sustain democracy in the face of inevitable political loss, Allen (2004) urges citizens to cultivate civic friendship—not an emotional affection, but a practice of recognizing and attending to the interests of those whose visions of the good life do not prevail in deliberation and decision-making. In part, this means that citizens learn to exercise restraint amidst political victory, and habitually seek opportunities for accommodation and compromise even when their political power and status would enable them to ignore others' priorities. "If we always act according to our own unrestrained interests," Allen contends, "we will corrode the trust that supports political bonds" (p. 137). This civic virtue of self-restraint seems particularly important for citizens, including many conservative Christians, who have a passionate certainty that their vision of the good life is exclusively superior to all others.

Citizens develop trust in the democratic process when they recognize that their fellow citizens strive to understand what is important to them and why. In addition, political losers need to have the assurance that the civic conversation will continue—that political loss is not final, and that they will still have the opportunity to be heard and hopefully understood. "A full democratic politics should seek not only agreement," Allen explains, "but also the democratic treatment of continued disagreement" (p. 63).

What are the educational implications of the need to cultivate civic friendship as an obligation of democratic citizenship? While classroom deliberation does not typically engage in political decision-making, the core practices that lay the groundwork for civic friendship should be cultivated as part of democratic dialogue. As explained earlier, a commitment to mutual understanding and developing the skills necessary to enable such understanding across profound ethical difference is central to such groundwork. When we better understand the central values and priorities of our fellow citizens, and the ways those values fundamentally shape their lives, we can appreciate what they may be giving up in the face of political loss or compromise.

While progress toward mutually held values and commitments is the deliberative ideal, depending on such comity to support political bonds is unrealistic. Our students should not be given the simplistic message that democracy depends on agreement; rather, they need to recognize that the strength of a democracy depends on how it handles inevitable and intractable disagreement. Students need to develop the commitment to ongoing conversation, and a willingness to exercise restraint and generosity toward those whose vision of the good life does not prevail. Such dispositions—and the skills to exercise them—will only be developed amidst an educational culture that emphasizes open-minded engagement with unfamiliar perspectives and a vision of citizenship that prizes informed compromise and accommodation as among its highest virtues.

The Tightrope of Civic Virtue

The argument of this chapter has been that room exists for religious students who bring ethical certainty to democratic deliberation, and that certain conceptual distinctions may prove helpful in enabling respectful dialogue. Granted, no easy formula exists, and these conceptual clarifications only open the door to the demanding work of appreciating unfamiliar ethical perspectives, demonstrating civic humility and cultivating civic friendship.

Ethical certainty presents challenges to civic deliberation, but careful coexistence is possible. "Open-mindedness towards new ideas does not at all imply that our present views are hesitant and wavering, only that they will need to be revised or rejected if they are found wanting" (Hare, 2006, p. 10). When public school teachers' pedagogical goals focus such revision or rejection on the civic realm, conservative Christians have room to participate without fear of frontal assaults on their faith convictions.

Liberal democracy relies on the distinction between the private and the civic. The civic realm has necessary and important boundaries, but must be informed by the private realm's deep ethical frameworks if our civic identity is to have any purchase and power in our lives together. For deeply religious citizens, this still-complicated relationship between private belief and public life together may still resemble a "high-wire act" doomed to failure (Callan, 1997, p. 37). It cannot be denied: the obligations of citizenship in a liberal-democratic society are substantive and demanding. How we help our students-as-citizens learn to navigate those challenges amidst the American reality of religious conviction and commitment will continue to shape our public square and our prospects for a shared life together.

Notes

1. The category of "conservative Christian" has blurry boundaries; oftentimes the term is used interchangeably with "Evangelical," since they both typically view biblical scripture as the highest source of insight and authority, asserting moral absolutes typically in tension with broader cultural norms and values. Christians who resist popular culture most fully are sometimes identified as "fundamentalist," and they often pair a separatist mentality with a desire to transform (or restore, in the eyes of some) the broader culture so that it reflects biblical precepts and priorities (Marsden, 1980; Ammerman, 1991; Smith, 1998). Like most ideological labels, however, the terms Christian conservative, Evangelical and fundamentalist risk obscuring more than they reveal. For the purposes of this chapter, the believer's fervent conviction that divine scriptural mandate trumps other sources of insight is most salient.

2. Throughout this chapter, I use the terms "political" and "civic" to denote the public realm of society, where we interact and coexist with citizens who may not share the private beliefs and commitments found in families, religious communities and so on. We engage in democratic dialogue with fellow citizens to work out the laws and policies of this public realm. (In political theory scholarship, the term "political" refers more narrowly to the involvement of government and state power.)

3. Obviously most teachers will be limited in their ability to engage students directly in such immanent criticism of a range of religious frameworks. That being said, the prevalence of religious teachers in K-12 schools (Kimball et al., 2009; Slater, 2008) suggests the potential for helping students gain an appreciation for the ways that the intellectual resources of their own ethical frameworks can challenge and sharpen their thinking. For example, the Calvinist theology of "common grace" (Kuyper, 1928; Berkhof, 1996) may provide helpful conceptual room for conservative Christian students to acknowledge the possibility of partial truths within broader ethical frameworks they might reject. The doctrine of common grace holds that God provides, among other blessings, the gifts of intellect and moral insight for all humanity; all truth is God's truth, and God sometimes uses "unbelievers" as the conduit for the expression of such truth.

4. This is not to say that public school curricula should not expose students to a range of views about the good life, and give students the opportunity to consider the values and priorities that shape their sense of meaning and purpose. But there seems a fine yet important line between providing those opportunities for students who are open to such exploration and teachers designing curricular experiences that require students to subject their own religious beliefs to critical analysis.

5. While religious students need to develop discernment regarding the appropriateness of religiously informed reasons, other students may need to avoid the error of categorizing religious reasons as inherently inferior to secular ones. Plenty of secular reasons are unreasonable, and many religious reasons are reasonable. As Richard Baer (1990) observes, "There are no reasonable epistemological standards that allow us to judge theological thinking as inherently inferior or less reliable than secular or nontheistic thinking" (p. 461).

References

Allen, D. (2004). Talking to strangers: Anxieties of citizenship since *Brown v. Board of Education*. Chicago: University of Chicago Press.

Ammerman, N.T. (1991). North American Protestant fundamentalism. In M.E. Marty, & R.S. Appleby (Eds.), *Fundamentalisms observed* (pp. 1–65). Chicago: University of Chicago Press.

Audi, R. (2000). *Religious commitment and secular reason*. New York: Cambridge University Press.

Baer, R.A. (1990). The Supreme Court's discriminatory use of the term "sectarian." *Journal of Law and Politics, 6*(3), 449–468.

Berkhof, L. (1996). *Systematic theology*. Grand Rapids, MI: Eerdmans Publishing Company.

Callan, E. (1997). *Creating citizens: Political education and liberal democracy*. New York: Oxford University Press.

Eberle, C.J. (2002). *Religious convictions in liberal politics*. Cambridge, UK: Cambridge University Press.

Gallup. (2012, Dec 24). *In U.S., 77% identify as Christian.* Retrieved from http://www.gallup.com/poll/159548/identify-christian.aspx

Hand, M., & Levinson, R. (2012). Discussing controversial issues in the classroom. *Educational Philosophy and Theory, 44*(6), 614–629.

Hare, W. (2006). Why open-mindedness matters. *Think, 5*(13), 7–15.

James, J.H. (2010). "Democracy is the devil's snare": Theological certainty in teacher education. *Theory and Research in Social Education, 38*(4), 618–639.

Kimball, M.S., Mitchell, C.M., Thornton, A.D., & Young-Demarco, L.C. (2009, July). Empirics on the origins of preferences: The case of college major and religiosity. Working Paper 15182. Cambridge, MA: National Bureau of Economic Research.

Kunzman, R. (2006). *Grappling with the good: Talking about religion and morality in public schools.* Albany, NY: SUNY Press.

Kunzman, R. (2011). Lessons in conversation: Why critical civic engagement requires talking about religion, and what that means for public schools. In J. Devitis (Ed.), *Critical civic literacy: A reader* (pp. 234–244). New York: Peter Lang.

Kuyper, A. (1928). *Calvin on common grace.* Grand Rapids, MI: Smitter Book Company.

Marsden, G.M. (1980). *Fundamentalism and American culture: The shaping of twentieth-century evangelicalism, 1870–1925.* New York: Oxford University Press.

Pew Research Center (2012, Oct 9). "'Nones' on the rise." Retrieved from Pew Research Center, Religion & Public Life Project site: http://www.pewforum.org/2012/10/09/nones-on-the-rise/

Rawls, J. (1999). *A theory of justice* (rev. ed.). Cambridge, MA: Harvard University Press.

Rorty, R. (1999). *Philosophy and social hope.* London: Penguin Books.

Slater, R.O. (2008). American teachers: What do they believe? *Education Next, 8*, 46–52.

Smith, C. (1998). *American evangelicalism: Embattled and thriving.* Chicago: University of Chicago Press.

Stout, J. (2004). *Democracy and tradition.* Princeton, NJ: Princeton University Press.

Weithman, P.J. (2002). *Religion and the obligations of citizenship.* New York: Cambridge University Press.

Williams, B. (1985). *Ethics and the limits of philosophy.* Cambridge, MA: Harvard University Press.

Zimmerman, J. (2002). *Whose America? Culture wars in the public schools.* Cambridge, MA: Harvard University.

9

CONTINUING THE CONVERSATION

Guiding Questions:

Why do we avoid religion and what are the consequences of avoiding it?
How has this book suggested we address religion in education?
What responsibilities do we have as we move forward?

I am a little bit embarrassed that the conversations captured in this book took me so long to begin. How many students have participated in my classrooms over the years, subject to a teacher who knew far too little about the role of religion in teaching and learning? I comfort myself with the reminder that I was at least thoughtful and reflective and willing to ask difficult questions in the face of uncertainty. But why was I not better prepared for the dilemmas I would face? It's a question that lingers in the cracks and crevices of this volume. It is not just my question. Something drove you to pick up this book—some curiosity, some experience you've had that left you wondering about religion and teaching, some professor who decided it was about time we put religion on the table for discussion. Kim's participants (Chapter 5) lament the fact that they have had so few opportunities to think and talk about religion as it intersects with their professional lives. My own experience at conferences and in schools confirms that educators long for space to think and talk about the issues included here.

Our aversion to talking about religion is, of course, not unique to teacher preparation and professional development spaces. Serious discussions of religion (not shouting matches) are rare in all walks of life. The absence of such discussion in the educational world, however, has particularly steep consequences—for teachers, for students, and (I believe) for our life together as members of the larger community.

Teachers who feel ill-prepared to handle dilemmas surrounding religion and teaching are more likely to do all they can to make sure such dilemmas do not arise. In a recent study I conducted of pre-service teachers' thinking about the role of controversy in the classroom, for example, a majority of participants at all levels reported that though they believed discussing controversial topics was a critical piece of social studies education, they didn't plan on touching certain issues. You might not be surprised to learn that abortion, same-sex marriage and gay rights were at the top of this list. These topics are, after all, hot-button topics outside of schools as well. What makes them particularly "hot" is that, for many of us, the position we hold on them is deeply entangled with our religious beliefs. But what was interesting to me was that religion *itself* was identified as a controversial topic by many teachers I interviewed. Lilly, an aspiring primary school teacher, claimed she would avoid religion in the classroom because,

> Religion is something people feel very strongly about and are very defensive about or jump to conclusions about . . . It's such a touchy, you know, it's like walking on poles, you have to be so careful with what you say . . . If it's taken home and you know, and if it's made aware to the parent, you know my goal and my means are not to offend anyone.

Jay, a secondary pre-service teacher, explained that he didn't feel knowledgeable enough to discuss religion with students. He said,

> There are so many religions out there . . . So what happens if you have a Muslim student in your class, or what happens if a couple Jewish kids ya know walk in, it's like I don't know about their religion. I try to, best I can, but I can't necessarily give you every bit of information about all the religions out there cause there is so many . . . I'd run into myself having to look stuff up. And I'd worry, "Did I just give the wrong information? Did I just lie to them?"

Travis echoed these sentiments, explaining, "I wouldn't want to offend anyone with my ignorance. People get offended way too easily. It's a sticky issue. I don't want to say the wrong thing."

Elizabeth, a secondary teacher candidate, said that she would probably avoid religion because students weren't likely to be mature enough to handle such a discussion. She stated:

> Religion is in the curriculum as part of early history, but the controversial aspects I would avoid. Seventh graders wouldn't be able to have the conversation because they are still too tied to their values—"You're wrong, I'm right." I don't want kids to leave my class arguing. It could turn into a fistfight.

Shannon, also a secondary pre-service teacher, claimed that she might bring up religion and religious issues. She also worried, however, about students' maturity level in talking about it and whether her students would "giggle and not be able to shut it off." Cara, who hopes to become a primary teacher, summed up participants' sentiment nicely when she said, "Religion. Quite frankly, discussing religion makes me uncomfortable."

Religion makes us uncomfortable and so we avoid it. Or does it make us uncomfortable because we avoid it? These aspiring teachers fear that their students won't be able to handle discussion of religion. They fear parents might be offended by or disapprove of how religion was addressed in the classroom. And they admit that their own knowledge—about religions other than their own, about what is legal, about how to justify their approaches—is severely lacking. Fear leads to avoidance. Avoidance leads to ignorance and more fear. What avoidance doesn't ensure, as is clear in the pages of this book, is that religion will stay out of the classroom. Religion is already very present—in the lived experience of teachers and students, in the curriculum, in the very fabric of schools themselves. Avoiding religion as a topic for conversation does not keep it off the table but only secures its place there as natural and right. Unfortunately, religion's taken-for-grantedness teaches young people powerful lessons about which religions and beliefs are "normal." Recall the second grader who said Hanukkah was "not as important as Christmas" or my friend's daughter who begged her parents to let her sit on Santa's lap or stay home from school the next day.

There are many reasons not to avoid putting religion squarely on the table. Teachers' failure to address religion in the classroom may teach students that religion is indeed a scary topic that should not be discussed. Teachers who avoid religion fail to provide students opportunities to reflect on how their religious understandings inform their thinking, and they give them little chance to learn how to engage respectfully with those whose understandings are different than their own. And so why are we surprised when at the slightest mention of a "hot topic," chaos ensues? Without opportunities to learn democratic living, students have few tools with which to navigate encounters with difference. Because religion constitutes one of the great points of division among people throughout time, it poses perhaps the greatest challenge to a people committed to democratic living. Avoiding it as a topic in schools is detrimental to society as a whole.

As adults self-select into increasingly homogeneous communities where they are less likely to engage in cross-cutting talk than ever before, and as the media grows more and more enamored with soundbites and mudslinging, where are young people to learn the difficult art of engaging with diverse others in responsible and respectful ways? I firmly believe in the potential of public schools to fill this gap. But if schools are going to be spaces for democratic living and learning, we have to do better. Much better.

The work begins in dialogue. It begins with a quest to better understand ourselves and others, with a willingness to pay attention. We must be willing to take up this conversation in our schools, communities and especially in our teacher education spaces. We must be willing to ask where and how religion is present in schools already. We must ask ourselves whether our schools and classrooms are spaces where individuals are safe to express their beliefs without being made to feel like outsiders.

My hope is that the vision of democratic education set forth in this book, and our brief interlude into law and ethics, can help to meaningfully ground and guide these conversations as we go. With mindfulness and mutuality in mind, we can move with intention, critically reflecting on what is and creatively imagining what could be. I am under no delusion that this volume has "cleared everything up" when it comes to religion in the classroom. Together, however, we have been introduced to a number of ideas for moving forward.

Kim, in her chapter on teachers, raised critical questions about the conflation of gendered, religious and secular narratives of primary school teaching. She pushed us to examine the "call" to love and serve, and to think twice about teaching as "natural" and innate, suggesting that these ideas about teaching may get in the way of our ability to develop authentic relationships with students. A good deal of work exists that attends to gender and primary teaching. What Kim's work adds to this body of scholarship is attention to religion as an aspect of teachers' identity development. Taking time to read this work, to reflect critically on the assumptions we hold about teaching, and how those assumptions may shape our practice in ways that facilitate or hinder democratic learning is important.

Simone's chapter helps us to see how students' religious understandings surface in the classroom—consciously, unconsciously and subconsciously. She encourages us to not only acknowledge students' religious understandings as they play out in their experiences of learning, but to intentionally "go fishing" for them so that they might become spaces for inquiry and understanding. Both of these chapters underscore the point that religion is ever-present in our classrooms as part of the identity and experience of those who spend time there. Both Kim and Simone call on us to talk—with each other, with students—in an effort to live more authentically together.

Keith, in his chapter on religion in the curriculum, advocates not only for teaching about religion, but also for teaching about religion in ways that honor its diversity and complexity, and facilitate students' understanding of religion's role in society. He pushes us to move beyond the major religions identified in our standards documents, to explore differences among those who claim the same religious identity, to consider how religious practices and beliefs shift over time and space, and to approach our teaching with critical awareness of how our own assumptions may shape our understandings. Furthermore, he encourages us to consider the social, political and psychological dimensions of religion as it figures into the lives of individuals in society. All of this, he argues, is necessary for understanding history, current events and for engaging respectfully and responsibly with others. Knowing that many of us feel unprepared to teach about religion, he offers a list of useful resources for deepening our own knowledge of religion and religions—and reassures us that we do not have to be experts—only inquirers.

In the most recent chapter, Rob goes right to the heart of what many of us fear the most—facilitating dialogue among students, especially when those students are sure they are right. Cue: Christina! If only I'd read Rob's work many years ago, I might have been a more competent teacher in the face of Christina's certainty. Rob describes four conceptual distinctions, which he argues are critical for helping students navigate religiously informed ethical disagreement. Teaching students to talk across difference involves facilitating their understanding of respectful engagement, of the difference between public and private spaces, of what it means to act with civic humility and of the power of conversation for bridging difference. If Keith's chapter aims to help us think about *what to* teach, Rob's chapter offers us an example of *how*. As issues of religion surface in our exploration of the past and present, we might do well to employ Rob's suggestions for engaging students in meaningful dialogue in ways that avoid leaving students angry, frustrated and disillusioned.

If there's one thing I've learned in my quest for understanding since that spring when I encountered Christina, it's that I cannot go it alone. Students like Christina, Matt, Rebecca; colleagues, parents and teachers at the schools where I spend time; family members, neighbors . . . It's in dialogue with diverse others that I have come to see how and why religion is present in schools, the consequences of its presence (and invisibility) for those *in* schools, and what sorts of barriers stand in our way of making change. My journey continues. Not a day passes that religion fails to cross my path—in the newspaper, in conversation, billboards, signs, advertisements, books that I read, movies that I watch . . . and I am reminded that of course religion is present in our schools. It is woven throughout the fabric of our lives—lives that necessarily enter the schoolhouse door with us.

It's because religion plays such a central role in the lives of many, because it has long played a powerful role in the social, political and cultural dimensions of our living together, that it must be unpacked. Knowing and understanding ourselves and others requires a willingness to see each other in all of our complexity and diversity, and to confront the ways those complexities and diversities interact in the public sphere. Talk is the bridge from assumption, stereotype, ignorance and fear to understanding, to seeing, to the building of authentic, mutual relationships.

I am grateful to my colleagues Kim, Simone, Keith and Rob for helping to break the silence around religion in the classroom. As always, their contributions to the conversation have pushed me to think even more deeply about the topics presented. I hope they have done the same for you. I hope that the time you have spent with us will inspire you to keep thinking—not only by yourself, but also in community with others. I hope that you will accept our challenge to carry the conversation into your school, your home, your neighborhood and your town. And I hope that what you learn there you will share with those of us still on a journey to understand, working to make schools places where democratic living and learning are possible. So talk and listen. Then speak up, speak out and speak back.

ABOUT THE CONTRIBUTORS

Keith C. Barton is Professor of Curriculum and Instruction at Indiana University. His research investigates students' understanding of history and society, as well as classroom contexts of teaching and learning and the history of the social studies curriculum. He has served as a visiting professor at Victoria University (New Zealand); the National Institute of Education (Singapore); and the UNESCO Centre for Education in Pluralism, Human Rights and Democracy at the University of Ulster. He is the author, with Linda S. Levstik, of *Doing History: Investigating with Children in Elementary and Middle Schools* (Routledge, 2011), *Teaching History for the Common Good* (Routledge, 2004) and *Researching History Education: Theory, Method, and Context* (Routledge, 2004).

Jennifer Hauver James is Associate Professor in the Department of Educational Theory and Practice at the University of Georgia. Her scholarship explores various dimensions of teachers' identity and lived experience as they influence their relationships with formal and hidden curricula, students, families and communities. She is particularly interested in the discursive, institutional and socio-political contexts that shape the possibilities we imagine for ourselves and for our students as educators in the United States. She is currently engaged in research that seeks to conceptualize young children's growth toward civic mindfulness. Her work has been published and presented in leading national and international venues. This is her first book.

Robert Kunzman is Professor of Curriculum and Instruction at the Indiana University School of Education. His research focuses on the intersection of religion, citizenship and education. He is the author of *Grappling with the Good: Talking about Religion and Morality in Public Schools* (SUNY, 2006) and *Write These Laws* *on Your Children: Inside the World of Conservative Christian Homeschooling* (Beacon, 2009). He serves as the Managing Director of the International Center for Home Education Research (icher.org).

Kimberly Logan graduated from the Department of Educational Theory and Practice at the University of Georgia in August, 2014. Her research interests include teachers' religious understandings and sense of purpose and the navigation of difference in democratic education. She is currently examining how standards-based reform can be used in teacher education settings to generate discussion on topics such as learner development, diversity and instructional practice.

Simone Schweber is the Goodman Professor of Education and Jewish Studies at the University of Wisconsin-Madison. She studies teaching and learning about genocide, how changes in labor conditions affect teachers' work, and religious education. She is the author of two books and many articles on each of these topics. She lives in Wisconsin with her two kids, a dog and a rabbit.

INDEX

agency 7–8
Allen, D. 86
American nationalism 34–5
assimilationist teaching 29

Barber, B. 7, 36
Baurain, B. 50–51
Baxter Magolda, M.B. 7
belief, study of as ethnocentrism 70–72
Britzman, D.P. 49
Brookfield, S.D. 6
Buddhism 71
Burke, K.J. 33, 34

calling and purpose in teaching 39–51;
    innate ability 45–6; teaching as love and
    care 46–7
certainty of belief and democratic dialogue
    79–87
children see students
Chinese folk religion 71
Christianity: and evangelism 70; influence
    on school system 31–5; as "normal"
    23–5
Christina 1–4, 10, 14, 17, 18, 20
Christmas trees 16
civic deliberation and ethical certainty
    79–87
civic education 5
civic humility 84–5
civic mindfulness 6–9
Clandinin, D.J. 41

Clark, Tom C. (Supreme Court Justice) 19
cognitive sophistication and civic maturity
    8–9
community identity and schools' religious
    practice 26–7
conflicts, religious 63, 74
Connelly, F.M. 41
consciously religious students 54–5
constitutional guidelines 15–19
cultural identity of community 26–7
curriculum issues 19–20, 61–77;
    ethnocentrism 69–73; religious diversity
    64–8; social, political and psychological
    dimensions of religion 73–6; and
    students' religious identities 54–8;
    teaching and leaning models 34–5

deficit discourse 28–30
democratic dialogue and ethical certainty
    79–87
democratic education 5–12
democratic living in schools 9–10
dialogical strategies 79–87
dissemination model of teaching 34
diversity of religion in the curriculum
    64–8
doubt, Christian students' worries about 18

Eastern religions 63, 70, 71, 72
Eberle, C.J. 84
Eckholm, Erik 25
Endorsement Test 16

Establishment clause of the First Amendment 15–16
ethical certainty and democratic dialogue 79–87
ethnocentrism and teaching of world religions 69–73
evangelism 70
exclusivity doctrine 69–70

Finding Common Ground (Haynes & Thomas) 21
First Amendment, US Constitution 15–19
First Amendment Center 21
Fraser, J.W. 31, 32
Free Exercise Clause of the First Amendment 17–19

Gerstle, G. 34–5
God on Trial (Irons) 21
Griffin, A.F. 18
guidance from God and calling to teaching 45–6

Hamachek, D. 39
Hand, M. 85
Hare, W. 87
Haynes, C.C. 21
Hinduism 71, 72
Holocaust lessons and Jewish students 54–5
Holy Ghost People, The (documentary) 63

individual autonomy 7
internal foundation and civic maturity 7–9
Internet resources 73
Ireland, Northern 63
Irons, P. 21
Islam 71

Jenks, C. 32
Johnston, B. 29
Judeo-Christian language in schools 33

Kimball, M.S. 48
King, Martin Luther 81
Kurtzman, David 15

Ladson-Billings, G. 29
language of education, Judeo-Christian origins 33
learning, role of religion 53–60
learning methods 34–5

legal issues 13–22; constitutional guidelines 15–19; resources 21; rights to practice belief 20; teachers' uncertainties about 50; teaching about religion 19–20; violations of the law 25
Lemon, Alton 15
Lemon Tests 15–16
Lemon v. Kurtzman 15
Levinson, R. 85
life events and religion 76
listening 7
literature as a resource 73
love of children and calling to teaching 46–7

Madison, James 15
Mann, H. 49
Memorial and Remonstrance (Madison) 15
mindfulness 6
moral education, role of teachers 27–30
morality, Protestant basis 32–3
Mormon students and teaching on wealth and poverty 58
mothering discourse 28–9
mutuality in democratic education 6–7

naming oneself 7
National Council for the Social Studies 21
Non-Public Elementary and Secondary Education Act 15
Northern Ireland 63

O'Connor, Sandra Day (Supreme Court Justice) 16

parents' rights 13–14
Parker, W.C. 7, 35
personal and professional identities of teachers 50–51
Polar Express Day 25
political dimensions of religion 73–5
Preskill, S. 6
Preston, J.A. 49
problem solving in the classroom 9–10
problems caused by non-Christian students 28–9
professional and personal identities of teachers 50–51
Protestant morality 32–3
psychological dimensions of religion 73–6
public and private realm distinction 83–4

realm recognition 83–4
reclaiming the self 7
religion: as controversial topic 92–3; in the curriculum *see* curriculum issues; role in student learning 53–60
religious beliefs of teachers: being tested 17–18; homogeneity 48–9; right to practice belief 20; and sense of calling 39–47
religious conflicts 73, 74
religious homogeneity of student teachers 48–9
religious identity of students: causing problems 13–14, 28–9; impact on learning 53–60
religious practice in public schools 25–6; Christian basis of school system 31–5; reflecting communities 26–7; *see also* legal issues
Republican Party of Texas 34, 35
resources: legal and ethical issues 21; overcoming ethnocentrism 73
respect 6–7, 82–3
Ricoeur, P. 8
Rorty, R. 80

schools: influence of Christianity 31–5; reflecting communities 26–7; religious practice in 23–6
secularization of Christianity 30–31
Segall, A. 33, 34
self, sense of 7–8
self-consciously religious students 55–7
sharing religious beliefs 20
Sherbert, Adell 17
Sherbert Tests 17
Sherbert v. Verner 17
Siddle Walker, V. 7–8

Snarey, J.R. 7–8
social dimensions of religion 73–6
Stout, J. 81
Strauss, V. 34, 35
strong internal foundation and civic maturity 7–9
structure of school timetable 31–2
student teachers: Christina 1–4, 10, 14, 17, 18, 20; concerns about legal issues 50; fear and doubt 17–18; religious homogeneity 48–9; reluctance to discuss religion 92–3; sense of calling 39–47
students: impact of religious identity 28–9, 53–60; rights to practice belief 20

teachers: as moral educators 27–30; reluctant to discuss religion 92–3; right to practice belief 20
Teacher's Guide to Religion in the Public Schools, A (Haynes) 21
teaching about religion *see* curriculum issues
teaching methods 34–5
Texas, Republican Party 34, 35
Thomas, O. 21
time structure of schools 31–2

unconsciously religious students 57–8
US Constitution 15–19

VanSledright, B.A. 34
Varghese, M.M. 29

Weithman, P. 85
White, K. 51
Winter Party 23–4
women and teaching 49
world religions in the curriculum 64–8